How to Make Sense

BY RUDOLF FLESCH

GRAMERCY PUBLISHING COMPANY • NEW YORK

TO KATIE

Acknowledgments

I am grateful to the following for permission to use copyrighted material:

To *Elementary English* for the quotation from the article "Linguistics and Reading" by Leonard Bloomfield (*Elementary English Review*, April-May, 1942).

To Charles Scribner's Sons for the quotation from the story "Death the Proud Brother" (from the volume entitled *From Death to Morning*) by Thomas Wolfe.

To Doubleday & Company for the quotations from the *Thorndike-Barnhart Comprehensive Desk Dictionary*.

R. F.

Contents

How to
Make Sense

1

A Sort of a Credo

Language is of the utmost importance to the whole practical and spiritual life of mankind.
—OTTO JESPERSEN, Language

How to make sense can't be learned from a book. All any book can teach you is how to think about yourself, your mind, your language, your way of expressing your thoughts, your successes and failures in communicating with your fellow men. Writing, reading, and speaking—communication, that is—can only be learned by practice—just like playing the piano, driving an automobile, or bringing up children. A book can give you pointers out of other people's experience; it can give you valuable facts about the materials you are dealing with; it can tell you in detail about a large number of things it would be an excellent idea *not* to do. It can lead you, the horse, to water, but it can't make you drink. The drinking part is up to you. So, as you read this book, keep reminding yourself of the true state of things: keep remembering all the people you know who make splendid sense without ever having read a book on the subject; and all those others who have faithfully gone through everything from Aristotle and St. Thomas Aquinas to the methodology of general semantics and advanced theory of group dynamics but still don't know what to answer when someone asks them, "Hot enough for you?"

But why should such an explanation be necessary anyway? How did we get to the point that people always expect a trick, a gadget, a formula, something that will teach them a precious secret of lifetime success in six easy lessons, fifteen minutes a day before breakfast? And how did it come about that this rags-to-riches success-book idea (once associated with such humble pursuits as fig diets or muscle-building) now has cropped up in the domain of culture? How to double your vocabulary and get rich . . . how to read twice as fast and land a vice-presidency . . . how to digest a hundred great books and become the life of the party . . . how to take a course in creative writing and make a thousand dollars on the side fifty-two weeks each year. . . . What *is* all this? When did it happen that the pursuit of happiness turned into a pursuit of words, sentences, and paragraphs? How and why did millions of grownup citizens of the United States suddenly discover that the way to salvation lay in the improvement of their English? Is this great new urge toward better-and-better communication just a fad? Or has someone somewhere made an important discovery? If so, what is it? Is it true, as some mathematicians say, that communication is the key concept of twentieth-century science? Is it true, as some philosophers say, that the study of language is at the bottom of all philosophy? Is it true that basically business consists of salesmanship and advertising, medicine of psychosomatics and bedside manner, law of draftsmanship and forensics, politics of speech-making, propaganda, and psychological warfare? Is it true that we live in a world where words are more important than things? Are those justified who feel that the true way to self-improvement is through better command of language? Or is it all a delusion and they would be better off if they took up yoga, nudism, or stamp-collecting?

Let's go slow in trying to find the answer to this riddle. First of all, let's face an obvious fact: Words *are* tremendously important today. Twentieth-century American society is a society based on the use of words. We are a nation of 160 million people who spend an enormous portion of their time in speaking, reading, and writing.

Never before in the history of mankind have so many people exchanged so many words. Day and night, from coast to coast, our country is filled with the reverberating sound of meetings, conferences, classes, training courses, salestalk, radio and television commercials, luncheon and dinner speeches, lectures, sermons, movies, shows, panel discussions, fireside chats, back-fence gossip, and just plain ordinary conversation. And when we don't talk or listen, we read and write. Newspapers, magazines, books, pamphlets, brochures, textbooks, training manuals, reports, instructions, house organs, sales literature, technical journals, workbooks, mystery stories, movie magazines, and of course the comics. How much of your day do *you* spend in oral or written communication? Six hours? Ten? Sixteen? Do you read the paper at breakfast? Do you talk business at lunch? How much of your work is speaking, listening, reading, and writing? How much of your leisure time? Think about it, and you will see that for all practical purposes we spend all our waking hours in communication. The intake and outgo of language fills our lives—

except when we are asleep, and even then we often dream of making speeches or reading books.

Life hasn't always been like that. Human history is the story of finding new means of communication. Look back from where we are now, and try to realize what has happened.

In the beginning, of course, there wasn't any language at all. The anthropoid ape made sounds with his mouth, to be sure, but those sounds didn't have any meaning; they didn't stand for anything. There was no symbolism, therefore no language. Then comes *homo sapiens*; the miraculous birth of language takes place and human history begins. Exactly how language was born, nobody knows; all that scholars can offer you are some pleasant, picturesquely labeled guesses. The "bow-wow" theory that says that language started with the imitation of natural sounds; the "ding-dong" theory that assumes some mysterious connection between sound and meaning; the "pooh-pooh" theory that says language began with short sounds of surprise, fear, and pain. My own favorite, the only one that feels right to me, is that of the late linguist Otto Jespersen who thought language began with emotional singing and chanting: "In primitive speech," he wrote, "I hear the laughing cries of exultation when lads and lasses vied with one another to attract the attention of the other sex, when everybody sang his merriest and danced his bravest to lure a pair of eyes to throw admiring glances in his direction." Or "suppose some dreaded enemy has been defeated and slain; the troop will dance round the dead body and strike up a chant of triumph, say something like 'Tarara-boom-de-ay!'"

Anyway, language begins somehow; human history begins. Things and events get names; information is passed on from one generation to the next; civilization starts.

Thirty, forty, fifty thousand years pass, and mankind takes another step forward. Man invents writing. For the next six or seven thousand years—that is, historically speaking, until very recently—writing and reading are a precious secret, known only to a tiny group at the very top of society. Literacy becomes the badge of office and leadership. Those who can make and decipher written records are in possession of the most powerful magic; a wide gulf separates them from the masses who live their lives by immediate experience and hearsay. They have access to history; they can control the events of the present—and perhaps the future.

And then comes printing, some five hundred years ago. And the slow, centuries-slow spread of literacy and education. And newspapers and magazines and books; the telephone; radio; television. And here we are today, with communication everywhere, always present, accessible to practically everybody. What was once the most precious possession of the leaders of mankind is all around you and me, cheap as dirt or water.

Of course, literary—and even plain literate—people are always inclined to look at history from their own, bookworm-ish angle. Their unspoken assumption is that everybody, at all times, was as literate, educated, and well informed as they themselves think they are. In their mind's eye is a historical never-never land where "everybody" read all of Dickens' novels, "everybody" followed daily communiqués of the progress of the Thirty Years' War, "everybody" talked at the dinner table about Galileo's latest theories. Somehow, anyone who writes occasional book reviews for the Podunk *Daily Ledger* thinks that in a previous incarnation he would of course also have been an intellectual—which means, an aristocrat, a priest, or one of the few idle rich.

The facts are otherwise. The overwhelming chances are

that your and my ancestors, or historical opposite numbers, were illiterate peasants, village artisans, butchers, innkeepers, or other ordinary folk whose communication hardly ever rose above everyday small talk. Their vocabulary was comfortably small, they hadn't read any of the great, medium, or small books, and their spelling, knowledge of grammar, reading speed, and technique of composition were happily deplorable. They didn't spend their lives with the perpetual din of words in their ears and the boundless sea of print all around them. The quantity of communication that filled their lives was immeasurably smaller than today, and without any undue nostalgia for a Golden Age of peace and quiet, I think they were happier.

Not that it matters though. An illiterate person may have been happy in an earlier age, but today he is practically certain to be severely maladjusted. No, we can't go back; we must go forward. There is no retreat from communication for any of us—unless you are one of the very, very few who are able, by temperament and circumstances, to go into the silences, retire to a South Sea Island, or become Trappist monks.

The rest of us have to grapple somehow with our twentieth-century, communication-filled lives. This is a world of words, and we must learn the command of words or perish. Words are *not* just words. We feel it, we know it in our bones: success, health, happiness in this world are inextricably tied up with language.

Look around you, look at the things that surround your daily life: houses, cars, clothes, food. To what extent are they made out of words? Think of it; think of the number of words that have gone into the production of each item in our civilization. The idea, the talking, the planning; the design

of the machinery, the engineering, the instruction and training; the management, the supervision, the reporting; the daily
operation, the checking, the bookkeeping; the correspondence,
the files; the government regulations, the taxes, the stockholders' meetings, the union negotiations; the selling, mer-
chandising, advertising; the shipping, the billing . . . How
many words does it take to produce a doll? To sell you a
bunch of parsley? To make a shoelace? Think of it. Think
of it long enough, and you'll feel that everything in this world
is just words. A highly one-sided view of the world, to be sure—
but an instructive one.

For it shows clearly that practically all jobs today are to
some degree speaking, reading, and writing jobs. Once upon
a time an illiterate deaf-mute could be a quite competent
member of society and, conceivably, a highly skilled laborer
or craftsman. But today most of us live by dealing with words.
Obviously that is true of managers, professionals, salespeople,
and clerks; but it's also true of those who run machinery or
supply personal services. Ours is a world where simple toys are
sold with elaborate instructions on how to assemble them;
where meals are ordered by writing down everything from
soup to nuts.

No wonder that words, words, words seem more important
every day for those who want to get ahead. The higher you
go—the better the pay—the more speaking, reading, and
writing and the less dirty work; in fact, dirty work in our
culture has become practically the same thing as work without words. And so it seems logical that the study of grammar,
spelling, vocabulary, public speaking, letter-writing has become
the road to success. Not long ago the economist Peter F.
Drucker insisted that the best preparation for any kind of

job is a college course in creative writing; some years back, the most widely read success book ever written, Dale Carnegie's *How to Win Friends and Influence People,* developed from a training course in public speaking.

Even that is not all. Words have become the key to success in the business world; but, as the title of Dale Carnegie's book shows, they have become the chief means of success in life in general. Better human relations—by the better use of words—are practical if you want to earn more money; but they are also widely recognized and advertised as the way to a happy home life, a secure standing in your community, and general peace of mind. Whether we realize it or not, we live on the assumption that words can and will make us happier.

Lately we have even begun to suspect that the wise use of words will increase our physical health. Psychoanalysis and psychotherapy—the treatment of mental disorders by protracted talk—have come into their own and have spilled over into psychosomatic medicine. Already we take it for granted that advertising executives get rid of their ulcers by regular visits to their psychoanalyst; and there is no longer any doubt that the psychosomatic cure by conversation can heal cases of asthma, arthritis and an extraordinarily long list of other ills. If talk on a couch in the presence of an analyst can cure you, will confession to a priest do the same? Or participation in group therapy meetings? Or *any* frank talking-out of your problems? Nobody knows but there are signs pointing that way, and the evidence for the amazing healing power of words becomes stronger every day.

And so, naturally, we are driven to the conclusion that language-learning, word-training is the most important thing we can do to help ourselves. This discovery is not new. It's as old as civilization; it's the thought underlying all education for a better life. Through the ages, those who could afford the best for their children gave them the best available training in the use of words. In all civilizations, the young aristocrats, the future leaders, the gentlemen-in-the-making were taught how to handle their native language, how to make speeches, how to read the classics, how to write prose and poetry, how to use and understand one or more foreign languages, how to be thoroughly at home in the world of words. The so-called trivium—grammar, rhetoric, and logic—was the core of liberal education in the Middle Ages; and to this day liberal education consists essentially in the training in verbal skills. Consciously or unconsciously, each one of us is convinced that a completely happy and healthy person ought to have read *Hamlet*, know that *believe* is spelled with the *i* before the *e*, and control the sinful urge to split infinitives.

But here we are, with literacy and education practically universal, and somehow or other we all feel that we never got the kind of education we ought to have in this word-ridden age. Some of us—still a small minority—went to college and were taught the liberal arts. But then again, nobody quite knows what a liberal education should consist of these days. Does it still include Latin and Greek? Few people think so any more. Does it include a reading of Freud, Marx, Nietzsche? Should every educated person know French? Or formal logic? Or economics? Who can tell? The only thing we all know is that no two people in the field of education ever fully agree. In the Middle Ages there wasn't the slightest doubt what an educated man ought to have studied; neither was there in China, through most of its history. But with us, you may spend an evening with two people of equally prolonged, expensive, and painful training in the liberal arts and find that their mental equipment has hardly anything in common. Consequently, the man who never studied Latin feels that this is what holds him back and envies the fellow who can mumble *Arma virumque cano* as the result of four years training; and the person who never read Milton vaguely feels that *Paradise Lost* contains the key to something or other—overlooking the fact that no one else he knows has read it either.

Those of us—the majority—who never had *any* kind of liberal education, old-fashioned, new-fangled or whatever, suffer of course from a much tougher case of this universal educational guilt complex. Our nerves twitch and twinge whenever someone mentions any of the hundreds of famous books we never read—whenever we are called upon to spell *harassed* or *parallel*—whenever we are about to say a word we have never said aloud before. Our universal education—based on the unattainable rule of "Be ye perfect" in grammar, spelling, pronunciation, vocabulary, and reading—has resulted in a universal neurosis. One way or another, all of us get nervous when we have to use words—which is all the time.

I know what you think at this point. You think all this is leading up to a diatribe against progressive education—"Our schools don't teach the fundamentals any more. . . . This is what comes from letting children do what they want. . . . Young people nowadays don't know how to read and write. . . ."—you know the kind of talk that immediately springs up whenever anyone in this country mentions the topic of education. Which side am I on? You have a right to know before you read any further.

Unfortunately I can't give you a simple answer to that perfectly legitimate question. I happen to be one of those people who feel that there is something to be said on either side—and that a great many of the arguments used on both sides are completely irrational.

To begin with, everybody's opinion on the subject of education—and everybody *has* an opinion about it—is colored by the kind of education he has had himself. Psychologists keep telling us that whatever happens to us in childhood gets lodged deep down in the unconscious and underlies all our thinking. Well, one of the important things that happen to everyone in childhood is that we go to school. So the schooling we have had unconsciously becomes the standard by which we judge everybody else's education. We got frustrated by spelling and can't spell properly to this day—so it's our considered opinion that weakness in spelling is a venial sin and shouldn't be taken seriously. We took a couple of years of Latin and went through Caesar and Ovid—so we insist that a certain limited amount of Latin is superbly valuable because it's an unexcelled method of teaching people to think. And so it goes. Ninety per cent of all the talk about education is an elaborate rationalization of the speaker's own educational assets and liabilities.

My own system of rationalization is somewhat extraordinary. It so happens that I was born and raised in Vienna and underwent the traditional Continental type of education, somewhat blunted by post-World-War-I progressive ideas. So I went to grammar school until I was ten and for eight more years to a *Realgymnasium*—a sort of public-high-school-plus-junior-college that dispensed, as no-nonsense compulsory subjects, eight years of Latin, six years of French, six years of world history (two complete rounds from the ancient Egyptians to just before the point where things have any bearing upon the present), eight years of mathematics (from the multiplication table right up to calculus and descriptive geometry) plus large gobs of chemistry, physics, biology, a year of Middle-High German, and a year of "logic and philosophical propaedeutics." After that, at eighteen, I went directly to Vienna University law school. (It's hard to convince anybody in this country that the institution of a liberal arts college is unknown on the European Continent. However, that's a fact. I repeat, I went from *Realgymnasium* to law school; there wasn't any place to go to in between.) Finally, years later, I got a second dose of education in this country, winding up with graduate work at Teachers College, Columbia University.

As a result of all that, I seem to have nothing but wrong responses whenever the talk around me veers in the direction of education. I have eight years of Latin in my system but never went to college; I read part of the *Nibelungenlied* in the original but am unfamiliar with some of the most hackneyed English and American poetry; and I am continually astonished by practically everything my children spend their time with in school. Just the other day my daughter, who is in fourth grade, came home with the news that they were now learning all about Australia. And so they were—including, of course, a vast number of things I had never heard about. But considering the fact that this was the first geographical unit they tackled in detail, I couldn't escape the nagging question "Why Australia?" They didn't start with England, or with Canada, or with Mexico, or even with the United States. No. Australia it had to be. The interior desert, the kangaroos, and Hobart is the capital of Tasmania. As I said before, I went to Teachers College and so I knew the theory behind it all perfectly well: if you can generate interest and the sincere wish to learn, it doesn't really matter where you start. And yet I—having "had" Australia three times as a boy, each time neatly wedged into the last hot week of the school year—I still can't help asking myself "Why Australia?"

Does that mean that I consider progressive education wholly bad? Of course not. The truth is that I don't remember anything I learned in school about Australia, or about a thousand other things I was taught according to traditional methods. My daughter, on the other hand, does stand a chance of enriching her personality and her future life with plenty of things progressive methods and good teachers will have given her. John Dewey and his followers believed in preparing children for real life and providing them with interesting, stimulating experience. Well, the generation that is now grown up did, on the whole, get this kind of education and it seems clear to me that they are better off for it. In fact, I firmly believe that progressive education is the explanation for a riddle that has plagued sociologists for the last six or eight years: the astonishing rise in the birth rate among educated people.

This startles you, doesn't it? Here is my theory: During World War II our birth rate went up; that's not surprising, it always happens during wars. After the end of the war the birth rate didn't drop to any extent, people kept on having more babies, and it became fashionable among middle-class families to have two, three, four, and five children. That's utterly surprising, completely contrary to all experience ever since the Industrial Revolution and the invention of birth control, and highly baffling to sociologists and population experts. According to all the rules, those statistical curves were supposed to go down, but instead they went up. What happened? I think what happened was this: The young middle-class couples who are now having babies are the first generation that has been brought up on progressive education. They are educated enough to use birth control if they want to, but their education has also given them the kind of personality that makes you bring a lot of children into the world even if you don't have to. They are trained for optimism, for tackling any kind of job, for learning from experience, for making the best of their environment. Conservative "book l'arning," as history shows, produces intellectual types living in city apartments—and dying out in two or three generations. Progressive education has given us millions of young middle-class couples, happily multiplying in suburban bungalows.

At any rate, that's my theory—which, in a roundabout way, accounts for the facts, whereas the experts can't account for them at all. Looking around me, I feel sure that progressive education has produced a happier young middle class, better adjusted to everyday twentieth-century life.

But unfortunately that's not the end of the story, nor the end of my argument. The years pass, and those young husbands and wives get older. Their children begin to grow up. The husband rises in his job, the family rises in the community, responsibility and even dignity sets in. Financial worries appear on the horizon—to stay there more or less forever—and life settles down. The day comes when husband and wife realize that they are now officially middle-aged. And then, more or less suddenly, the problem of education comes up again. By now, the actual subject matter learned in school has been thoroughly forgotten, and the personality training that has worked so well during the twenties and early thirties has more or less spent itself. Crises and emergencies have arisen, all sorts of setbacks have come and gone, and the great lesson that any situation can be tackled by work and intelligence has lost most of its force.

Meanwhile it turns out that some important elements of education seem to be missing. The husband is ready to step into an executive job, but has the uneasy feeling he hasn't got the vocabulary to hold his own in the new environment. He isn't good at writing letters and memos, and has trouble with his spelling. He is frightened when he has to make speeches. He never gets around to reading the books people are talking about, let alone the classics, most of which are just names and titles to him. He also knows that his reading is painfully slow, and a slow reader in an executive position is in an awkward fix.

The wife—who in our system has to keep up with the Joneses *and* with the career of her husband—runs into the same problems. According to statistics, she probably has had less formal education than her husband to begin with; so her handicap is even greater. She tries to keep her end up in women's club meetings and such—and usually, being blessed with a woman's insight that these things don't really matter, settles down to a happy acceptance of her own pet misspellings and the fact that serious nonfiction bores her stiff.

And that, I think, is the true state of affairs. Progressive education—just like our automobiles, washing machines, shoes, and overcoats—is practical, good-looking, does an excellent job, and gives you a happy feeling while it lasts. But it doesn't wear well. Instead of lasting you a lifetime, as an education should, it goes to pieces when you're about thirty-five or forty. Then, contemplating the problem of how to get through the rest of your life, you realize that you don't know enough solid, basic stuff, that you haven't read the right books, that you are way below par in speaking and writing. Twenty years after, you see that it might have been a good idea after all to spend the years from six to sixteen or from six to twenty, in just plain drill in spelling or the multiplication table, or in learning a seemingly useless foreign language, or in reading a lot of boring books.

But now it's too late. And so you, like millions of other Americans, look for a quick remedy that will fix you up in no time. After all, that's standard procedure. "After thirty-five," if we run into "irregularity" (as the copywriters so neatly call it) we buy a box or a bottle of this-or-that and expect "immediate relief." Why not apply the same principle to educational troubles? Why not indeed? The parallel is only too clear. We can't re-live our lives to correct faulty eating habits and we can't go to school all over again to get ourselves the kind of education that will stick. So we buy a book; we take a course; we spend fifteen minutes a day.

And that's why we have a country full of grownup people suffering from a mental rundown feeling and searching perennially for a quick remedy. They take courses in writing, they buy books on vocabulary building, they train for rapid reading, they tackle prescribed lists of Great Books. Does it help? Why yes, it helps in the same way that any pill or patent medicine helps: it's a shot in the arm, it raises the spirits, for a while it makes you feel awfully good. And then a reaction sets in, somehow the stuff doesn't take any more, those additional words don't seem to do anything for you, you discover that your reading rate is slowing down again to a lazy trot, you start bravely on the first chapter of Erasmus' *In Praise of Folly* or

The Federalist Papers and the bloom is suddenly off. So you switch. You try another well-advertised brand of remedial education—forums on current affairs, say, or a book on semantics—and after a while you get bogged down in *that*.

Am I trying to disparage all efforts to improve your mind? Of course not. It's all to the good. It all helps, up to a point, and anyway you can't re-live your somewhat misspent youth, as I said before. But let's face the fact that all those "remedial" efforts are poor substitutes for the real thing. A bottle of vitamin pills is not the same as a basket full of apples, and a home exercise gadget is not the same as climbing a mountain. The trouble with our current methods of relieving educational ills is that they are all artificial, synthetic, ready-made for mass consumption, quick sale, and quick replacement.

So if, at thirty-five or forty, you want to do something about gaps in your education, don't shop around for the quick-formula, immediate-results type of thing. It won't work. The only thing that will work in the long run is the kind of training you should have gotten as a child but didn't. It will go slow and it will take lots of time—evenings, Saturdays, Sundays. It will consist of learning how to write not by a quick formula but by the old-fashioned device of steady practice; of increasing your vocabulary not by ten words a day but by days and weeks and months of reading and listening to unfamiliar words; of reading not Great Books or Best Sellers or Books-of-the-Month but simply books that will exercise your mind instead of relaxing it—and keeping on reading such books one after another after another.

Old-fashioned? I suppose so. But after all, the subject of this book is How to Make Sense, and you can hardly expect me to neglect the thinking of several thousand years on that venerable theme. It's an old-fashioned subject all right, and if you want novelty you'll have to content yourself with the novelty of applying plain common sense to such up-to-date matters as vocabulary-building, speed-reading, and human-relations training. My feelings about many of these things are like those of the little girl in Andersen's fairy tale who couldn't help observing that the Emperor had no clothes on. I just don't believe in tricks or patent medicines, and if that's what you are after, my book is not for you.

And now I have to go into a somewhat personal matter. I have to confess that I am the begetter of something called a readability formula, a mathematical gadget designed to improve your writing. How come? How can the author of a writing formula have the effrontery to attack other educational prescriptions? Give me a couple of pages and let me explain.

To begin with, my formula isn't the kind of formula that is usually associated with writing. The dictionary contains several definitions of the word and my formula is *not* "a rule for doing something, esp. as used by those who do not know the reason on which it is based" (such as the famous 5-W formula for writing news reports or the so-called "AIDA" formula for salestalks and ads) but it's the mathematical kind of formula: "a rule or principle, frequently expressed in algebraic symbols." In other words, my formula is not a gadget but an equation. If you feel that your writing or speaking is not up to par and apply my formula, it won't make you feel better like a drug but it will tell you what's wrong like a thermometer.

I first worked out my formula in 1943, then revised it in 1948, and finally developed a completely new formula, which you will find in this book. Several of my earlier books dealt with these formulas and gradually there started something like a readability movement. People in journalism, advertising, personnel work, and all kinds of other professions took up the idea of measuring the length of sentences and words and began to pay attention to readibility standards in their writing. Soon, however, mysterious forces got to work and before I knew it I was saddled with the responsibility for the cut-and-dried, patent-medicine kind of formula—the one I thoroughly dislike and despise. Somehow or other the more subtle elements of my formula got lost in the shuffle and only a mechanical count of words and syllables remained. On top of that, people took the statistical averages I had found and turned them into fixed writing rules. One nice day I was introduced to the editor of a publishing house that used my formula. "Ah, so *you* are seventeen-word Flesch!" he said with a broad grin—making me feel exactly like the man who was asked whether he had stopped beating his wife.

The fact remains that my formulas are designed to measure readability. They are *not* meant to make you into a successful speaker or writer overnight. Nothing will do that—neither vocabulary-building nor reading a hundred classics nor limiting your sentences to seventeen words.

And what *will* help you make sense? As I said before, the slow, old-fashioned things. In particular, since it's communication we are talking about, daily practice in communication. Not the learning of words that have nothing to do with your daily life; *not* the reading of books you can't relate to your own experience. Instead, start where you are. Beginning writers are taught to write about things with which they are familiar. The same goes for you. Improve your writing by putting some extra effort into your ordinary reports, memos, correspondence.

Don't force yourself to break into the short-story field by hook or crook; instead, write that letter to an old friend you should have written six months ago, and make it ten pages of good, meaty reading. Don't read another book on vocabulary, or human relations, or semantics; instead, pick your favorite debating topic and have it out with your brother-in-law once and for all, even if it takes until four A.M. Your job, your family, your friends are your proving ground for learning how to make sense.

I have given you fair warning. The first few chapters of this book will deal with some of the current superstitions in the field of language, just to get them out of the way. The rest of the book deals mainly with basic, essentially simple things: your choice of words, the rhythm of your speech, the relation between you and your audience, how to get ideas.

Finally, there remains the all-important fact that language is not all there is to communication. We exchange words with each other, but we also exchange looks, expressions, gestures, movements, actions, attitudes, all sorts of meaningful behavior. Speaking, reading, and writing are only the conscious, surface part of communication; but according to the psychologists, it's the underground, unconscious communication that counts. Can emotions be conveyed without words? Of course they can, and "emotional contagion" is now a well-known fact. Can thoughts be conveyed without words too? Perhaps. Some psychologists are working on the problem and William James, the most famous of them all, went so far as to say:

> Out of my experience, such as it is (and it is limited enough) one fixed conclusion dogmatically emerges, and that is this, that we with our lives are like islands in the sea,

or like trees in the forest. The maple and the pine may whisper to each other with their leaves, and Conanicut and Newport hear each other's foghorns. But the trees also commingle their roots in the darkness underground, and the islands also hang together through the ocean's bottom. Just so there is a continuum of cosmic consciousness, against which our individuality builds but accidental fences, and into which our several minds plunge as into a mother-sea or reservoir.

And so, perhaps, all our efforts to make better use of words are as nothing compared to the insight that no man is an island and we are all brothers, members one of another.

2

Is Grammar Necessary?

> *Those who have written English Grammars have been taught Latin; and either unable to divest themselves of their Latin rules, or unwilling to treat with simplicity that which, if made somewhat of a mystery, would make them appear more* learned *than the mass of people, they have endeavored to make our simple language turn and twist itself so as to become as complex in its principles as the Latin language is.*
>
> —WILLIAM COBBETT, English Grammar (1820)

A LARGE PART OF YOUR LIFE WAS SPENT IN learning English grammar and usage.

What did you get out of it? How often do you use your precious knowledge of moods and tenses, participles and gerunds, demonstrative pronouns, and subordinating conjunctions?

The obvious answer is, Never. You speak, read, write all day long, but throughout your adult life you haven't spent a single second in deciding whether to put a verb in the indicative or the subjunctive, or in exercising a choice between a definite and an indefinite article. Grammar is something you learn, promptly forget, and dismiss for the rest of your life.

Why should this be so? How did it come about that a considerable part of your school learning was devoted to something so utterly useless? Once you start to think about it, you immediately realize that here is one of the biggest mysteries of our civilization.

Grammar—the grammar of your native tongue—is the only thing you study *after* having learned how to use it. In everything else the sequence is, Ignorance, Learning, Application. In grammar it's the other way round. You start with knowledge and application, and then you learn.

You learned how to walk by the delightful process of taking steps holding on to the hands of your mother or father, and then graduating to taking the first, second, and third step alone. Similarly, you learned how to talk by saying *Mommy*, *Daddy*, and *doggie* and proceeding to such feats as *I want ice cream* or *Me sound asleep*. Did it ever occur to anyone to teach you walking all over again, explaining carefully the proper sequence of muscle movements and the exact angle at which to bend your knees? Of course not. But you *were* taught, laboriously and for years on end, that in constructing the sentence *I want ice cream* you were using the first person singular, nominative case of a personal pronoun as the subject, and the present indicative, active voice of a verb as the predicate, whereas in saying *Me sound asleep* you committed the double, unforgivable crime of putting the personal pronoun in the objective case and uttering a sentence fragment in the bargain.

The vast majority of mankind would consider this procedure completely crazy and incomprehensible. You learn

how to use words; then you use them. What else is there to
study? Ask an African Negro or a South Sea Islander—anyone unspoiled by Western habits of thought—and he will
look at you in astonishment. He has learned how to master
his native tongue; as far as he is concerned, grammar doesn't
come into it. Correctness, purity of speech—what does it all
mean?

Of course with us this whole idea is so ingrained that we
are embarrassed and disconcerted when someone raises such
a question in polite society. Children must learn grammar
because otherwise they would grow up without having learned
grammar; we must have standards of correctness in speech so
that we can avoid grammatical errors. It's completely illogical;
the whole thing falls to pieces after five minutes of consecu-
tive thought. And yet we all hang onto it for dear life as one
of the mainstays of our educational system.

How did it all start? The story has long been well known.
The study of English grammar was invented in England in
the early eighteenth century. "Many of the writers on language," writes Professor Robert C. Pooley in *Teaching English Usage,*

> were retired clergymen or country philosophers who,
> though possessing some skill in the classics, had no con-
> ception at all of the history of English or the methods of
> linguistic research. Too frequently their statements on Eng-
> lish usage were the products of false philology or of per-
> sonal prejudice. Moreover, the philosophy of the age was
> inimical to scientific research in language; the prevailing
> conceptions of language were (1) that language is a divine
> institution, originally perfect, but debased by man; (2) that

English is a corrupt and degenerate offspring of Latin and Greek. The first theory gave rise to the application of reason and the analogy of language in an effort to restore English to its pristine glory; the second resulted in corrections of English idioms to make them conform to classical models. The actual usage of English was ignored or despised by all but one or two of the writers of this age.

Soon textbooks on grammar began to flourish.

One of the most influential of the eighteenth-century writers on language was Bishop Lowth, whose *Short Introduction to English Grammar* appeared in 1762. In 1795 an American named Lindley Murray wrote a grammar, nearly all of which he copied from Lowth. Murray's book enjoyed an enormous popularity; it is estimated that over a million copies were sold in America before 1850. Murray's successors copied freely from his book, so that the direct influence of Lowth persisted well into the latter part of the nineteenth century.

I am still quoting Professor Pooley's book *Teaching English Usage*. I'll bring the story up to date by adding a sentence from a speech Pooley made in 1950:

The eighteenth-century tradition of English grammar continues almost unchanged, leaving an ever-widening gap between the sound conclusions of our liguistic scholars and the archaic method of teaching the structure of our lan. guage.

And that's where we are now. Having been brought up on the unscientific ideas of those eighteenth-century retired clergymen and country philosophers, we fervently believe in good grammar and correct usage. An English teacher to us is someone who has drunk deep from the well of the laws and rules of language—strange and unfamiliar to ordinary mortals —and can show us how to mend our sinful ways. Poor infinitive-splitters all, we try to put our best foot forward in the presence of a member of the National Council of Teachers of English and ask shyly whether punishment for saying *It's me* is still on the books.

In more pronounced cases we write letters to newspaper editors or otherwise do our bit to uphold the grammar-and-usage dogmas. Not long ago the Bacardi rum company announced in an ad that "a Bacardi old-fashioned contains less calories than a lamb chop, a Bacardi cocktail less calories than a boiled egg." Did people protest that the logic was specious or that the argument was immoral? Not at all. Instead they wrote in, in droves, that the copywriter should have said "fewer" instead of "less" and was corrupting the language of poor, innocent school children, already gravely endangered by exposure to television commercials and the comics.

And just recently the worship at the shrine of the good Bishop Lowth produced an incredible comedy of errors—the kind of thing a fiction writer wouldn't dare to put into a story because it's much too improbable. One nice day in the spring of 1953 New York State Assemblyman Philip J. Schupler, a Ph.D. and principal of the summer session of Brooklyn Preparatory School, was reading the State Surrogate Court Act of 1920. His eye fell upon the heading of Section 140. It read: "Who to be cited thereupon; contents of citation." Dr. Schupler shuddered. His soul cried out that the first word of the heading should be "Whom." Stirred to his depths, he arose in the next session of the legislature. He brought in a bill to change the indecently exposed *who* to a nice, well-behaved *whom*. The legislature of the State of New York voted. The bill was passed. In due course, it came before Governor Thomas E. Dewey and was signed. But the governor, disturbed, vented his feelings in a memorandum:

> The grammatical error occurs only in a section heading, and aside from the question of precise usage there is no problem as to clarity or construction of the statute. Although I am impressed by the laudable erudition, the bill in all other respects is wholly unnecessary and represents a waste of several hundred dollars in taxpayers' money. . . . I am constrained to approve it, though I thoroughly disapprove the practice.

End of the story? Not quite. Newspapers reported the incident and after several weeks Dr. Schupler, the 206 members of the New York State legislature, and Governor Dewey learned that they had all overlooked a small but essential piece of information: "Who to be cited" had been grammatically correct all the time, even by the standards of the venerable Bishop Lowth, who would never have dreamed of putting the subject of a passive verb in the objective case. At the expense of several hundred dollars the State of New York had *created* a grammatical error where there had been none before.

The point I am driving at is that the study of correct grammar and usage is the oldest and most widely known of those mechanical, artificial, completely unscientific linguistic remedies that I talked about in my first chapter. We have a vague feeling that we could do better in our speaking and writing;

the first thing that comes to our minds is that we ought to do something quick to avoid making grammatical mistakes. So the most widely used "communication pills" are books and courses in "better English." "Thousands are handicapped by poor English—and don't know it!" cries a full-page ad for one of those courses; and "Do You Make These Mistakes in English?" says the headline on another. Do people respond to this approach? They certainly do, by the millions. The ad headed "Do You Make These Mistakes in English?" has run unchanged for decades and is famous among advertising men for its universal, never-failing appeal.

And what do people get when they sign up for one of those courses? You guessed it: the heritage of the immortal Bishop Lowth. *Whom* for *who*, *fewer* for *less*, and all the rest of the eighteenth-century linguistic revelation. Will that help you become a vice president and get into the country club? I doubt it.

Of course I don't mean to say that all grammar and usage that is being dispensed nowadays is of the Bishop Lowth variety. There *has* been progress. There have been linguistic scholars and members of the scientifically oriented wing of the English teaching profession, led by such men as Robert C. Pooley, whom I quoted earlier, and Porter G. Perrin, author of the widely used college text *Writer's Guide and Index to English*. Professor Perrin has also contributed excellent, up-to-date usage notes to the *Thorndike-Barnhart Comprehensive Desk Dictionary*, published in 1951. Here are some examples:

> In formal English *whom* is always used as the accusative form. In informal English when the *who* stands before a verb or preposition of which it is the object, *who* is the

generally accepted form: *Who do you introduce to whom? No matter who you meet, the first thing you mention is the weather.*

In formal English careful distinction is kept between the auxiliary *can* when it has the meaning of ability, "being able to," and *may* with the meaning of permission: *You may go now. He can walk with crutches. You may if you can.* . . . In informal and colloquial English *may* occurs rather rarely except in the sense of possibility. . . . *Can* is generally used for both permission and ability: *Can I go now? You can if you want to. I can go 80 miles an hour with my car.* This is in such general usage that it should be regarded as good English in speaking and informal writing.

Lot, lots of. The colloquial uses of these words, appropriate in speech and in some informal writing, are avoided in formal writing: Colloquial: *We tried a lot of different kinds.* Formal: *We tried a good many different kinds.* Colloquial: *He has lots of friends. . . a lot of money.* Formal: *He has many friends . . . a good deal of money.*

As you can see from these examples, the typical modern— or even ultramodern—reference book gives you the Bishop Lowth type of grammar and usage side by side with the grammar and usage you use yourself—or *would* use hadn't your impulse been checked by learning the "correct" way of saying things. You take your choice, those books tell you. In informal speaking and writing you go by *your* rules, in formal speech and writing by those of the bishop.

What does that mean? Where are you supposed to draw the line? What is formal, what is informal? If the decision is left to you, you probably figure that informal speech and writing is the kind of talking you do around the house, plus the note-to-the-milkman type of writing. Everything else, you suppose—talk and writing at the office and to strangers—must be the formal kind and that's where you have to use the *whom, may, a good many* type of language. That's tough, but you decide you'll do your best. Tomorrow morning you will start. You'll pick up the telephone and say: "With whom am I speaking? May I talk to Mr. Smith? Thanks a good deal."

But that isn't at all what modern English teachers have in mind. To them, formal and informal means something entirely different. If you look up the word *informal* in the *Thorndike-Barnhart Dictionary*, you'll find Professor Perrin's explanation:

> Informal English is the typical language of an educated person going about his everyday affairs. It lies between the uncultivated level on one side and the more restricted formal level on the other. It is used not only for personal affairs, but for most public affairs—of business and politics, for example, except in strictly legal matters—for most newspaper and magazine articles, for the bulk of fiction and drama, for a good deal of poetry. In the last generation or so it has come to dominate English writing, partly in reaction against the more elaborate style of the nineteenth century. . . . Formal English is passed on chiefly through reading and so represents in many respects the usage and style of the preceding generation of writers; informal English lies closer to speech.

Which means, in plain words: Informal English—*your* kind of English—is what you are supposed to use all the time; formal English—the Bishop Lowth kind—is of as much practical use to you as a top hat. You might as well forget it.

If that's so, why is all the information you get about up-to-date, scientifically acceptable usage carefully labeled "informal English," to be sharply distinguished from "formal English," where all the old rules apply in full force? Why is this useless, once-in-a-blue-moon language still being taught in even the most modern books? Why does the *Thorndike-Barnhart Dictionary* hide the truth about grammar and usage in an inconspicuous note under the word *informal* where no reader would ever look for it? Why is Bishop Lowth's outmoded, unscientific grammar and usage still being served up to all and sundry under the deceptive label "formal English"?

You'll admit that these are reasonable questions to raise. But I can't expect you to get as excited about them as a young college professor engaged to teach normal, twentieth-century English to freshmen and finding them filled to the brim with all the nonsense about "formal English" and its glory. In October, 1951, one of those men exploded in the pages of *College English*, the official organ of the National Council of Teachers of English. It's impossible to say it better than he did, and so I'll yield the floor at some length to Mr. Tom Burnam of the Colorado State College of Education. The following are quotations from Mr. Burnam's outcry:

> As many of you are aware, most students are acquainted with two kinds of English: *real* English, the kind people they know use, and the other kind which a creature whom I call Miss Higginbotham tries to impose in the classroom. Now, Miss Higginbotham may be a pleasant person in many ways. But, oh, the damage she has done by the time I encounter her charges in my college classes! This morning I

asked my students, among whom are the usual I-done-its and it-ain'ts and we-wases, to tell me what they remembered most clearly of the English they had learned up to now.

I said, "Were you taught always to say *can* for ability and *may* for permission?" Vigorous nodding of heads, none more vigorously nodded than that of poor Bramwell, the worst of the I-done-its. I asked, "Did Miss Higginbotham (my students know her) tell you never to split infinitives?" Even more nodding, Bramwell again giving a passable imitation of a sunflower in a stiff breeze. I said, "Did she forbid prepositions at the end of sentences?" Bramwell *et al.* assured me that she had.

"What else did she teach you?" I asked. "*Anything* else." Silence. "Can't you remember a single thing about your previous work except *can* and *may* and split infinitives and prepositions at the end?" I asked. No, they couldn't. All they could remember was three rules that don't exist.

Well, so what? Perhaps split infinitives and so on *aren't* really very important; still, does it hurt a student to know these things? Yes, I think it does. What a great many teachers of English still do, it seems to me, is to enforce upon the student what can only be called a dream-world: a dream-world where no "careful speaker or writer" ever says "awful" or "swell" or "lousy" or "Aren't I?" or even "Nuts!". . . .

I do not think I exaggerate in placing much of the blame for the college teacher's troubles squarely on Miss Higginbotham's shoulders. She is the one, I am convinced, who first introduces her students to that miasmic distinction between "formal" and "informal" English. . . . She leaves her students with the impression that full-dress is the proper costume for breakfast, lunch, dinner, the athletic field, the classroom, and the grocery store. . . .

I am convinced that even among professors "formal" English accounts for less than 1 per cent of their language activities. . . . I cannot waste my time training students in elaborate devices concerning an activity to which they will devote, at the most, less than 1 per cent of their time. Besides, I'm not worried about their "formal" writing. They all know how to write formally, thanks to Miss Higginbotham. What *I* can't get them to do, in their themes or elsewhere, is to write in a lively, interesting, *informal* manner. Yet why shouldn't they have trouble writing easily and informally? Miss Higginbotham has told them it's sinful.

Poor Mr. Tom Burnam, out in Greeley, Colorado, fighting against the forces of majestic, centuries-old superstitions! "Formal English" is just another fortification in the formidable defense-in-depth that protects the disciples of Bishop Lowth. And even that is not the last rampart. Behind it there looms up the mighty bastion called "educated usage" or "standards of the best speakers and writers." Even in *informal* speech and writing you are not supposed to do what you feel like: you are told to observe the example of your betters and do likewise.

For this is the last, up-to-the-minute word the "liberals" among the English teachers have given out: the old, rigid, eighteenth-century rules are dead; long live the new rules of "educated usage."

Go back through the past few years of the *English Journal* and you will find, in almost every monthly issue, the "Current English Forum," conducted by the leaders of the progressive wing of the profession: Harold B. Allen, Adeline C. Bartlett,

Margaret M. Bryant, Archibald A. Hill, James B. McMillan, Kemp Malone, Russell Thomas. This valiant band of professors is determined to convince the country's high school English teachers of the superiority of colloquial usage. And how are they tackling that impossible-looking job? They use research, data, statistics. Look at all the distinguished *who*-users, they cry; observe how the literary great eschewed the subjunctive; see how many respectable people split infinitives. Do you teachers still believe in the dogmas of the 1700's? Let's show you the facts and figures and you will come over into our camp.

And so the liberal grammarians for years and decades have been looking into every nook and cranny of old and new writing to find examples of so-called "incorrect" usage. With tremendous industry they have managed to find *who's, it's me's,* and *he don't's* here, there, and everywhere. By the thousands, they have collected specimens like these:

"Everybody has a way of their own." (Jane Austen)

"Tyranny is one of those evils that tends to perpetuate itself." (Lord Bryce)

"Trying to sit up, the whole room had reeled." (Hervey Allen)

"You had ought to tell me that." (Robert Louis Stevenson)

"One don't begin with writing straight off." (Rudyard Kipling)

What does all this prove? To the true believer in strict grammar, I'm afraid, it doesn't prove a thing. So, he would admit, famous writers and speakers occasionally make mistakes; let's forgive them. Let's not play up those little lapses and hold them up as shining examples to our youngsters who are in the process of learning what's right and wrong. All those research data are blandishments of linguistic devils, temptations meant to lure us from the strait and narrow path. A dangling participle is a dangling participle, no matter how many may be unearthed from the classics; without correct grammar the English language will perish.

This is a strong argument—strong enough to have called forth a recent editorial in the *English Journal,* pleading for more research, more data, more statistics to find out once and for all which of those examples are isolated "mistakes" and which represent genuine trends. There must be a way, the editorial said, to establish how most educated people talk most of the time; if all the evidence collected so far is not enough, let's have more. Let's settle it all by statistics.

And there the matter stands. The battle lines are drawn, and sooner or later we shall know. If it turns out that infinitive-splitting is prevalent among 63 per cent of "educated speakers and writers," then we'll all buckle down and split them, by golly, from there on; if only 39 per cent are found to be practicing participle-danglers, then we shall abstain from that ugly habit and return to the golden rules of Bishop Lowth.

Absurd? Yes, I think it's absurd. And yet, this is the logic of the present thinking in grammar and usage. The battle cry is "Do what the majority does!" In the final analysis, the scientific rules of grammar and usage consist in following the herd.

What's wrong with that? you ask, and I can't blame you. The following-the-herd principle is thoroughly entrenched in our society. It is often called "keeping up with the Joneses" and even more often, with a proud air of authority, "adjustment." Ask any psychologist and he'll tell you that people who say "I ain't" are maladjusted and need remedial English to escape serious personality troubles.

I don't think that's the final answer. I don't think America, "the land of the free," is destined to become the world's largest do-what-everybody-else-does country. "Adjustment" is the battle cry of those who want to escape from freedom and responsibility, as the psychologist Erich Fromm has pointed out in a famous book. We are *not* all meant to drive a Buick as soon as six people out of ten in our block drive a Buick. We are *not* going to arrange our sex life so as to have the proper number and kind of "outlets" found prevalent among people of our station in life by the eminent Dr. Kinsey.

And so, in grammar and usage, we shall sooner or later recognize the statistical approach as a snare and a delusion. We won't return to a belief in the divine inspiration of good old Bishop Lowth, but we won't submit either to rules of grammar and usage by majority decree. Democracy doesn't mean that the minority simply disbands. Our constitution guarantees free speech—and that logically ought to include the freedom of following the demands of your grammatical conscience.

Of course if unconventional grammar makes you feel uneasy, change your habits by all means. There is no doubt that even fifteen minutes a day of eighteenth-century grammar, ridiculous as it may seem, will pay dividends for you: all efforts toward self-improvement are helpful if they succeed in enlarging the powers of your mind. But don't expect more than that. Don't expect that a course, a textbook, an outside authority will ever solve your daily language problems for you. How to speak and write—how to adapt yourself to the communication demands of each day, each minute, each audience, each situation, each purpose—will always be for you to decide. You have to be your own grammarian.

This is a harsh doctrine, I know, since it puts the responsibility all on your own shoulders. Is there no help and guidance at all then? Is there no book, no authority that you can rely on, and fall back on whenever you are beset by doubts? Do you have to go through life fighting the battle of the split infinitive each time the problem comes up? Do you have to live solely by your own, home-made grammatical rules?

No, you don't. Because it so happens that there is one book, and one only, that gives you advice on grammar and usage that is neither of the dusty, musty eighteenth-century type nor of the statistical, "appropriate-in-informal-usage" variety. That book is A *Dictionary of Modern English Usage* by H. W. Fowler, published by Oxford University Press in 1926. Fowler wrote his masterpiece when he was seventy years old. What he says about questions of grammar, usage, vocabulary, and style is always wise, original, based solely on his deep understanding and sincere love for the English language. Some of Fowler's views are too British for us Americans; some of his facts and observations are out of date. But on the whole his book is still superbly useful here and now. It is incomparable; there isn't any book on the English language that can be mentioned in the same breath.

Modern English Usage has had a tremendous influence on writing in England, the British Commonwealth, and the United States. In this country its indirect influence is even greater, since it was the bible of Harold F. Ross, the late editor of *The New Yorker*. Much of our best current prose is modeled after *The New Yorker*, and so owes its grace and beauty eventually to Fowler.

Fowler's book has become so famous that recommending it is now a platitude. Just to do it a little differently, I shall therefore simply add a few quotations. (And if there is any other book on English usage from which you can quote charming epigrams, I'd like to see it.)

When we say *damn*, it relieves us because it is a strong word and yet means nothing; we do not intend the person or thing or event that we damn to be burnt in hell fire; far from it; but the faint aroma of brimstone that hangs forever about the word is savoury in wrathful nostrils.

Of course, as the herald of an out-of-the-way fact that one has just unearthed from a book of reference, is a sad temptation to journalists.

A potato is a tuber, but the fact should be left in the decent obscurity of agricultural textbooks.

It stands to reason is a formula that gives its user the unfair advantage of at once invoking reason and refusing to listen to it.

Distinction, as a literary critics' word, is, like *charm*, one of those on which they fall back when they wish to convey that a style is meritorious, but have not time to make up their minds upon the precise nature of its merit.

That's the kind of guidance you will get from Fowler. You may not always agree with his recommendations; but you will never be able to dismiss him without doing quite a bit of thinking of your own.

For the rest, as I said, you will have to be your own grammarian. Are you then supposed to speak and write as the spirit moves you? Are you supposed to go by feeling and by ear? Yes —provided that your feeling and your ear have not been perverted by "correct" grammar to play you tricks.

I shall give a simple example of what I mean by this. Just

yesterday I was reading an article on jet planes in the *U. S. News*. One of the interviewer's questions was this: "Why hasn't our Air Force ordered a prototype of a jet military transport like the British have done?"

The word *like* is used here as a conjunction. This is a usage strongly condemned in all grammar books and not considered acceptable even in informal writing. Reading the sentence, I winced. My inner voice told me—by the unmistakable sign of wincing—that here was an example of bad usage.

And yet, what is the real significance of my wincing? Exposed to a certain type of language stimulus, my nervous system reacted in a certain way. How come? Obviously because at some time in the past it was conditioned to react that way. I didn't wince because *like* as a conjunction is absolutely, by and of itself, "bad grammar"; neither did I wince because I was born with a tendency to wince whenever I see that construction in print. I winced because the followers of the late Bishop Lowth had managed to build this pet dogma of theirs into my nervous system.

In other words, rigid and unsurmountable dislike of a particular speech form is actually a kind of slight neurosis, an "informal usage phobia" produced by instruction in "correct" grammar and usage.

Some time ago I presented this point of view to a group of English teachers. Naturally, they shuddered. I have thought about the matter since, trying earnestly to arrive at a conclusion that would be less repugnant to English teachers' feelings. However, as far as I can see, what I said was the exact truth: "correctness" in grammar and usage is a sort of neurosis.

Let me prove this with an analogy. Suppose you notice that it always gives you a slightly queasy feeling to ride in elevators or stay for some time in other small enclosures. You decide to do something about it and go to a psychiatrist. The psychiatrist takes half a minute to diagnose your ailment as a slight case of claustrophobia and proceeds to cure you by psychoanalysis. You spend a number of hours on a couch, going over your childhood experiences, and in due course it turns out that your claustrophobia goes back to an incident when you were five years old and had to spend two hours in a closet. The psychiatrist rejoices in having found the trauma, shows you that you don't need to be frightened of that closet any more, and after some time you are able to ride in elevators just like everybody else.

Now suppose you take the same approach to grammar and usage. You notice that you wince whenever you hear or read a sentence containing the word *like* used as a conjunction; you decide to get rid of that nervous reaction; you go to a psychoanalyst. The analyst puts you on a couch, you rehash your childhood experiences, and—lo and behold—you find that Miss Higginbotham in sixth grade frightened you by calling the use of *like* as a conjunction a horrible bad habit that would make the rest of your life utterly miserable. The psychiatrist tells you that this was a trauma, assures you that *like* as a conjunction is perfectly normal and nothing to be frightened of, collects several hundred dollars for the treatment, and sends you home. Pretty soon you are able to read the *U. S. News* and similar reading matter without any disturbance whatever.

Is this a fanciful idea? Not at all. There is no reason to believe that it couldn't happen. Sensitivity to "incorrect" grammar is an acquired habit and in extreme cases of "informal usage phobia" it *is* a neurosis. If you can't talk to an Italian-born cab driver without suffering from his mistakes in English grammar and usage, then you are ill-adapted to current American life and, to that extent, not quite normal. You want to learn what is considered correct and standard? By all means do so. But use that knowledge to become free—free to feel at home in the English language everywhere and with everybody.

I shall conclude this chapter with three splendid examples of such freedom. They were chosen at random; each example is grammatically "incorrect"; each is a proud assertion of the right of each individual to suit his language to the time, the place, and the occasion.

The first example is from E. M. Forster, the author of *Passage to India,* who is today generally considered the dean of English letters. One of Forster's essays—a brilliant piece on anonymity—begins with the words:

"Do you like to know who a book's by?"

This is a gem. Not only did Forster put the preposition *by* at the end—a practice universally condemned by grammatical fuddyduddies—he also chose the "incorrect" *who* over the "correct" *whom.* And yet what could anybody do to improve that sentence? "Do you like to know *whom* a book's by?" Sounds all wrong. "Do you like to know by whom a book is?" Even worse. "When you read a book, do you like to know by whom it is?" Terrible—dull, uninspired, pointless.

No. "Do you like to know who a book's by?" Let's just look again and admire.

Second example: The other day I read an interview with Mark Van Doren, one of our leading poets and literary scholars. I quote: "Everybody's mind is full of poetry and ideas all the time, but they don't know it."

They refers back to *everybody,* a lack of agreement in num-

ber that enrages the Miss Higginbothams. So what should
Mark Van Doren have said? "Everybody's mind is full of
poetry and ideas all the time, but *he* doesn't know it"? Quite
so; but that sounds like a prosaic scientific observation. It
isn't what Mr. Van Doren meant at all. He had no data on
the subject; he just knew. He wasn't writing a treatise; he said
what he thought was the truth. And besides, if you say *he*,
there is a faint air of exclusion of the female sex about the
sentence—as if women's minds were *not* full of poetry and
ideas all the time. Surely that isn't what Mr. Van Doren
meant to say, is it? If there's any difference between the sexes
in this respect, he probably would say it's the other way round.
"Everybody's mind is full of poetry and ideas all the time, but
they don't know it." Right. More than correct. True.

Finally, a beautiful example of a split infinitive. Here is
Walter F. Kerr, drama critic of the New York *Herald Tribune*,
reviewing a Broadway play called "My Three Angels." It's
about three convicts doing time in the French Guiana penal
colony, who set about to help the local storekeeper's family
overcome various misfortunes. "In the process," Mr. Kerr
writes, "they are not only willing to doctor the store's books,
to snatch fowl for an impoverished dinner table, and to bait
a trap for the girl's reluctant lover. They are perfectly prepared, if need be, to gently and tastefully dispatch the villain
of the piece to his eternal reward."

Now "to gently and tastefully dispatch" is doubtless a split
infinitive. The felony is even compounded by the insertion of
three words rather than one between *to* and *dispatch*. Again,
should Mr. Kerr have avoided the "mistake"? Should he have
written "They are perfectly prepared, if need be, gently and
tastefully to dispatch the villain of the piece to his eternal

reward"? Obviously this would have been a change for the worse since the words "gently and tastefully" would then seem to refer to "if need be," which would turn the meaning of the whole sentence upside down. Or should Mr. Kerr have solved the dilemma this way: "They are perfectly prepared, if need be, to dispatch the villain of the piece gently and tastefully to his eternal reward"?

No again. If you write "They are perfectly prepared, if need be, to dispatch," you create the impression that the dispatching is done quickly and brutally—which is, of course, just the opposite of "gently and tastefully"; and these two words, inserted afterwards, will never quite repair the damage.

What then? Recast the whole sentence to avoid the necessity of committing a split infinitive? Yes, that's exactly what a stickler for eighteenth-century grammar would say. He would sacrifice a delicately constructed piece of precisely balanced English prose in order to pay homage to the memory of Bishop Lowth. With neurotic glee he would destroy the product of Mr. Kerr's fine craftsmanship because he has lost the faculty of appreciating it.

Let's turn our back on such an unhealthy point of view. Let's enjoy again this split infinitive, this lovely piece of superbly chiseled grammatical intaglio: "They are perfectly prepared, if need be, to gently and tastefully dispatch the villain of the piece to his eternal reward."

Yes, Mr. Kerr splits a mean infinitive. Go and do likewise—if you can.

This is where I meant to end the chapter, but on reading it over I see that it needs a sort of postscript. Since I clearly disagree in these matters with those on the right, on the left, and in the middle, chances are that many readers will misunderstand what I was trying to say.

So, for the record, let me add: I do *not* believe that all instruction in grammar and usage is worthless and should be abandoned forthwith. I *do* think and firmly believe that grammatical "correctness" is an eighteenth-century superstition; that "formal speech and writing" are practically nonexistent in ordinary twentieth-century American life; that "educated usage, followed by the best writers and speakers" is largely a myth. But there *is* such a thing as scientific grammar, based on the work of such men as Jespersen, Curme, and Fries, and there is an intelligent approach to usage, as exemplified in Fowler's wonderful book.

During the past ten years or so, I have talked with many hundreds of grownup Americans about problems of grammar and usage. I found that they fell into two groups. The older generation was brought up on the doctrine of correctness, vaguely remembered such things as pronouns and conjugations, and asked where I stood on *It's me* and the split infinitive. The younger generation had never learned *any* grammar to speak of, couldn't define a split infinitive if their life depended on it, and consequently suffered from a vague but painful grammatical inferiority complex. Neither of them, I am convinced, would benefit much by the fifteen-minutes-a-day type of instruction in "correct grammar"; but both of them would gain by a prolonged, extensive study of the modern Jespersen-Curme-Fries type of grammar or the habit of dipping into Fowler ever so often and then browsing in it for hours. This way they would *not* reach "good English" by a shortcut —which is impossible—but they would in time gain the grammatical freedom I was talking about.

And the children? Why yes, they too should learn scientific grammar and the basic facts and even niceties of English usage. They should be told that expressions like *He don't want none* and *like I says* are frowned upon by many people in our society, and they should be trained in handling such problems with skill and detachment.

And maybe in time another generation of Americans will grow up that will handle the English language with calm assurance and freedom from fear.

3

Why Read Faster?

A truly great book teaches me better than to read it. I must soon lay it down, and commence living on its hint. . . . What I began by reading, I must finish by acting.

—THOREAU, Journal

A FEW DAYS AGO I RECEIVED A LETTER FROM A large industrial corporation, which began: "We are extremely interested in practical ways and means of improving the skill of our engineering and supervisory personnel in handling the heavy individual reading, writing and dictating loads."

The letter was a symptom of the tremendous interest in reading improvement that has suddenly taken hold of American business. The reasoning is obvious: Executives spend a large portion of their time in reading; most of them are slow readers; let's speed up their reading and we'll save an enormous amount of very expensive time. And so, courses in reading are the latest wrinkle in American personnel management.

There is much irony in this. For years, decades, generations our schoolteachers have tried to make children good readers, to instill a love of books in them, to bring them to the point where they will enjoy and appreciate Shakespeare, Chaucer, Dickens, Tennyson, Browning, the Lake poets, Gibbon's *Decline and Fall*, and Burke's *Speech on Conciliation*. For years, decades, generations children have resisted those efforts, adolescents have abandoned books as soon as they got out of school, and adults have treated reading on a par with etiquette, piano playing, and crocheting. Now at last the poor neglected schoolteachers come into their own; reading is again recognized as important. But have Americans come around to the idea that books are good for the soul? Not at all: they are "interested in practical means of handling their heavy reading loads." Instead of taking up the classics at long last, they want to have more time for memoranda, trade journals, letters, and reports.

Why is it that executives have trouble with their reading? Basically the answer is the same as with other aspects of our education: In early middle age, when the demands upon verbal skills are rising, it turns out that the fundamental education we got back in school isn't good enough. Grownup Americans are poor readers because they were never properly taught. Reading courses for executives are the result of what happened —or didn't happen—in first and second grade.

There is not the slightest doubt of where the trouble lies. Our reading instruction is based, and has been based for over a hundred years, on the so-called recognition or whole-word method: the child looks at the letters C A T and is shown or told that this letter combination means "cat"; he looks at A R E and is told that this means "are." In other words, he is not taught to *read* words at all, but is simply coached in the habit of guessing their meaning. Language scientists, the only professionals competent to deal with the problem, have long said that this is stupid; but our educators—the people actually in charge of what to do to children while they are a captive audience in the classroom—have stubbornly refused to listen and have continued to teach reading by their own dim lights. Result: Executives who can't get through their mail.

Before I go into what to do about that situation, I want to spend a couple of pages in setting down, in detail, the scientific method of teaching a child to read. This won't be much help to yourself, I know. But you may have small children—as I have. And like all parents of small children that I have ever met, you may be eager to know how I made my eldest daughter into a perfect reader before she entered first grade. Here it is: it's as simple as ABC. My source is the late Professor Leonard Bloomfield of Yale, who was the leading language scholar of our age. I am quoting his paper "Linguistics and Reading" (*Elementary English Review*, May, 1942):

> The first step . . . is the recognition of the letters. We say that the child *recognizes* a letter when he can, upon request, make some specific response to it. . . . The conventional responses to the sight of the letters are their names, *aye, bee, see, dee,* and so on, down to *zee. . . .*
>
> Our first reading material must show each letter in only one phonetic value; thus, if we have words with g in the value that it has in *get, got, gun,* our first material must not contain words like *gem,* where the same letter has a different value; similarly, if we have words like *cat, can, cot,* our first material must not contain words like *cent.* Our first material should contain no words with silent letters (such as *knit* or

gnat) and none with double letters, either in the value of single sounds (as in *add, bell*) or in special values (as in *see, too*), and none with combinations of letters having a special value (as *th* in *thin* or *ea* in *bean*). The letter *x* cannot be used, because it represents two phonemes (*ks* or *gz*), and the letter *q* cannot be used, because it occurs only in connection with an unusual value of the letter *u* (for *w*).

Our first reading material will consist of two-letter and three-letter words in which the letters have the sound-values assigned at the outset. Since the vowel letters are the ones which, later on, will present the greatest difficulty, we shall do best to divide this material into five groups, according to the vowel letter.

The work of this first stage is all-important and should be continued until the pupils are very thoroughly trained. Nonsense syllables, such as *bem, bap, mim, mip*, should be included. Words unfamiliar to the child, such as perhaps *van, vat*, should not be avoided; they should be treated as nonsense syllables or, if there is time, accompanied by a very brief explanation of their meaning.

Short sentences of the type *Nat had a bat* can be used at this stage.

The second stage takes up regular spellings in which double consonants and other digraphs appear in consistent uses, e.g. *ll* as in *well, th* as in *thin, sh* as in *shin, ch* as in *chin, ee* as in *see, ea* as in *sea, oa* as in *road, oo* as in *spoon*. If a very few words of irregular spelling are introduced at this stage (e.g. *is, was, the*), it is possible to devise connected reading of reasonably varied content.

The third stage takes up words whose spellings may be called semi-irregular, for example the type of *line, shine, mile, while,* or the type of *bone, stone, hole, pole.* At this stage, also, two-syllable words whose spelling is consistent with the other materials, can be taken in: *winter, summer, butter, sister* (but not, for instance, *father, mother, brother*). A small set of the commonest irregular words (pronouns, forms of the verbs, *be, have, do,* and *go*) is included because it enables us to give extended readings of connected text.

The last stage takes up irregularly spelled words, such as *father, mother, night, all, rough, cough, tough.* . . . At this last stage we use only familiar words which are needed for reading.

And that, ladies and gentlemen, is the sum and substance of the reading instruction method devised by America's greatest student of language. As I said, I used it to teach my oldest girl and found it as easy as pie to work out reading matter she enjoyed, like *Anne has a big bed* or *Anne drinks a mug of milk* or *Rigi is a big pup* (Rigi is our two-hundred-pound St. Bernard). Anybody can do the same; and anybody would be a fast competent reader now if he had been exposed to the Bloomfield method at six.

But let's leave that sad topic and let's return to you—the adult who wants to improve his reading. Let's begin with a basic question: Are you solely interested in speed or do you want also better comprehension, a surer grasp of facts, a way of getting "more out of your reading"? Is it intangibles you are interested in or just the hands on the clock?

Probably your answer will be that you want both; and you suspect this means you want to have your cake and eat it too. If you learn to read faster, it seems logical that your reading won't go as deep; you will pay for the time you save by getting less stuff transferred from the page into your head.

Luckily, however, that isn't so; reading, like everything else that has to do with the mind, is thoroughly paradoxical. It has been proved over and over that faster reading will get you *more* instead of less—more understanding, more clarity, more grasp of the subject. The reason is this: When you read a word in a sentence, you first assign to it a *provisional* meaning in your mind, a meaning that may be reconsidered and corrected when you have come to the end of the phrase, the sentence, or the paragraph. A word in context is never fully understandable by itself; paradoxically, every word you read must be understood in the light of the words that come before *and after* it. Therefore, the faster you read, the better you are able to attend to that process of correcting and understanding by hindsight; the slower you read, the more danger of sticking to a wrong provisional meaning until it's too late. If you read two hundred words a minute, like an average American adult, the words will be too widely spaced in time to shed much light on each other; if you read at a rate of four hundred words, those second two hundred words that you have crammed into one minute's reading will make the meaning of the first two hundred twice as clear.

So it *will* profit you to speed up your reading and you won't have to sacrifice comprehension to speed. And how can you train yourself to read with more speed? You may have heard or read about various gadgets—speed reading machines, films, and so forth. The principle back of all those devices is the same: you learn rapid reading by forcing yourself to read more rapidly. To do this with mechanical aids will doubtless help you; to do it together and in competition with others will help you too; but there's no reason why you can't do the same thing all by yourself and with no more equipment than a wrist watch. Simply time your reading (roughly estimating the number of words on a page) and then force yourself to go faster—and faster—and faster.

The joker with this—as with all other ways of changing your habits—is that your new skill may not last. At first you will doubtless make great progress; after a while, though, things will settle down, and if you don't watch out you'll soon be back where you started. What can be done about that? you ask. The answer is, Nothing—except for the old-fashioned method of sticking to the job day after day. Rapid reading, I'm sorry to tell you, is a lifetime job—like dieting, brushing your teeth, or paying taxes. Or like walking, to take the simplest example of all. If you care to, you can start tomorrow on a program of doubling your customary walking speed. You time yourself; you walk twice as fast to and from the office; you get an exhilarating sense of accomplishment; your blood circulation and your digestion improve; you feel fine. Two, three, six weeks pass—and your lifetime habits prove far stronger than your brand-new resolutions. Before you know it, you are back at the old trot.

As you see, I don't want to disparage the virtues of rapid reading at all. I just want to warn you. Inertia is one of the basic forces of the universe.

There are all sorts of other things you can do about your reading—all valuable. You can train yourself to look for essentials and skim or skip the rest. You can learn to concentrate better and shut out distractions and noises. You can make it a habit to read with a pencil; you can underline, make marginal notes, talk back to the author. Above all, you can remind yourself of the great truth that only reading with a purpose will do you any good. Ideally, to "get the most out of your reading," you should read everything with the utter absorption you give to a love letter or the single-mindedness with which you search for a number in the telephone book.

Reading, after all, is something you *did* learn in school (although not as well as if you had been taught by the Bloomfield method). You know how to do it, only you don't do it properly—because you are lazy, uninterested, absent-minded, because you ate too much last night, because you are worried about the grocery bill, because all sorts of things go on in your life that prevent you from being at the top of your form. There are no miracles. The simple secret is that if you care enough to keep up the effort you can learn how to read better; if you try to cure yourself with a fast-acting drug, the effect will pass.

But enough of that. In my effort to tell you about the facts of educational life, I seem to be getting awfully moralistic. Let's pass on to something else—to the underlying question of *why* you should improve your reading.

There is a simple answer to that question: You should improve your reading so that you can easily read *Silas Marner* by George Eliot.

No, I am not joking. I am just drawing a logical inference from well-known, established facts. These are the facts:

1. Educational experts agree that the highest purpose of reading is the study of literature.

2. The most important works of literature are required reading in our schools.

3. The book most widely required in our schools is *Silas Marner*.

So, in essence, you learn to read so that you can read *Silas Marner*.

At this point, I have to make the wildly unrealistic assumption that you have never heard of *Silas Marner*. Let's assume that you are a person from Mars, assigned to a survey of the literature teaching that goes on in American high schools. You descend to Earth, assemble the necessary statistics, and find that practically all high schools in the country agree in forcing students to read this book by a certain George Eliot. (George Eliot, you gather, is an Englishwoman called Marian Evans who has been dead for quite some time.) So you settle down to studying that bible of American English teaching and discover the following:

Silas Marner is a weaver in the remote English village of Raveloe, fully engaged in the pursuit of avarice. Another character in the book is a certain Godfrey, who is courting a girl named Nancy, although somewhat hampered by the fact that he is secretly married to someone else. One evening that secret wife, accompanied by an equally secret daughter of toddling age, sets out and walks to a clump of bushes near Silas Marner's cottage. There she conveniently dies of an overdose of opium. The toddling child immediately toddles to Marner's cottage. She finds the door open, due to the fact that Silas Marner is given to brief trances, during which he always unconsciously opens his front door. The little girl settles down in front of the fireplace, Silas Marner returns to consciousness and closes the door, notices the light falling on the child's golden curls, and immediately thinks it is his heap of gold coins, which was stolen several weeks before by the little girl's uncle, Dunstan, who fell with it into a stone pit and killed himself. Soon, however, Silas Marner realizes his mistake . . . etc. etc.

Now of course it's very easy to make fun of a melodramatic English novel of the 1860's. So what? you say. So Silas Marner is something of a fairy tale; that doesn't change the fact that it's an acknowledged masterpiece and a good thing for teen-agers to read.

In answer to that let me acquaint you with certain facts that I dug up before writing this chapter. (Not only that, I also read *Silas Marner* for the first time in my life; after all, research is research.) The facts are these: *Silas Marner* is *not* one of the universally acknowledged great classics. It is true that George Eliot figures on some of the lists of "best books" (though not on all by any means), but the work usually included is her novel *Adam Bede*. In the opinion of most experts, *Silas Marner* was not typical of her best work. Brander Matthews, in his list of one hundred best English novels, cites four of her other books but not *Silas Marner*. The co-operative reading list of the National Council of Teachers does include it but calls it, with obvious disdain, "a sentimental story." The famous University of Chicago list of Great Books (I'll come to that in a minute) has no place for George Eliot at all. In short, *Silas Marner* is a minor work by a Victorian novelist whose standing among the world's greatest writers is somewhat doubtful.

Why bother then? Because, I repeat, it's the book that practically all our high school students are forced to read. Naturally, they hate the very sound of it. They moan and groan. They don't want to have anything to do with the rustic types that populate Raveloe, with the salvation of the miserly weaver, and with the whole syrupy story. But read it they must. Occasionally a harassed teacher confides her *Silas Marner* troubles to the *English Journal* and tells about what she did to get that impossible book down her students' throats. One of them, in a Mississippi high school, let her students stage a radio quiz program about the book; another, in Indiana, let them work on a map of Raveloe. What ingenuity in the face of impossible odds! I bow in admiration to those two unsung heroines of our educational system. But even such desperate measures can't convince me that *Silas Marner* deserves to be the crown jewel of our schools.

I realize that it's hard to be objective about these things because English teachers, not content with giving us "informal usage phobia," have also filled us with a "classics compulsion." We can't help it. Long ago we all acquired the nervous habit of considering certain famous books "musts"—not musts in the sense that we read them every day, but musts in the sense that everybody is supposed to have read them at least *once*. Of course none of us has actually read the whole list from Aristotle to Zarathustra, but the polite thing is to pretend that we have. If someone mentions Plato's *Republic*, we nod knowingly as if we kept the book at our bedside and dipped into it every night. To admit our ignorance is like announcing that we walked out of the house this morning without brushing our teeth.

It's a little easier for me to talk about these matters because I went to school in Vienna. Of course I did the usual amount of required reading there too, but since Austria is a German-speaking country and English wasn't included in the curriculum, the list of titles was entirely different. So—having gone through Lessing, Kleist, Moerike, Theodor Storm, Grillparzer, Stifter, Schiller's *Taucher*, and Bürger's *Lenore*—I am able to admit without nervous discomfort that I spent my formative years entirely untouched by Tennyson, Browning, Longfellow, Washington Irving, *The Vicar of Wakefield*, and

Lamb's *Dissertation on Roast Pig*. No doubt all these things are nice to read; so are the German classics and, for all I know, the French, Spanish, Indian, and Chinese ones. But to go on the assumption that everybody has to be baptized by total immersion in a certain group of these books is an exaggerated notion, to say the least. Reading *Silas Marner* won't make you an educated person; neither will a reading of all the prose and poetry our schools happen to teach.

But, you say, what about the Great Books? What about all those book discussion groups springing up everywhere, what about the famous list of one hundred books, what about the big Great Books program that has stirred up so much interest? Do I mean to say the whole idea is wrong? Am I trying to discourage you from applying yourself to the books that contain mankind's basic ideas?

Let's first of all look at some facts. The Great Books program—or movement—is the brainchild of Robert M. Hutchins and Mortimer Adler, who were long connected with the University of Chicago. It goes back to a course in the Great Books taught by John Erskine at Columbia during the twenties; and that, in turn, was the successor of a course taught to the A.E.F. in Biarritz during the First World War. Before that, there was a long succession of lists of best books, drawn up by various literary men as a sort of parlor game. The first such list, it seems, was made by the English writer Sir John Lubbock in 1887. None of those lists or courses was ever offered with the idea that reading all the books would give anyone "an education"; the notion seems to have sprung up as a sort of folklore.

What do you get when you join one of the Great Books discussion groups? Well, you get the list of hundred books drawn up by the Chicago educators. If you spend about two weeks on each book—a pretty steep schedule, you realize—it will take you about four years to get through the course, not counting vacations, sick leaves, and occasional falls from grace with a best seller or a mystery story. Your program will include *Huckleberry Finn* and Shaw's *Plays Pleasant and Unpleasant*, but otherwise you won't have much fun. You'll study the *First Ennead* by Plotinus, Calvin's *Institutes of the Christian Religion*, the *Outlines of Pyrrhonism* by Sextus Empiricus, and the *Fundamental Principles of the Metaphysic of Morals* by Kant. You will also read Euclid's *Elements of Geometry*, Lavoisier's *Elements of Chemistry*, and selections from Hippocrates' medical writings of the fourth century B.C.

Do I sound discouraging? I mean to be. I think the Hutchins-Adler group is on the wrong track. What started as an inspired—and inspiring—idea of John Erskine (who obviously was one of the greatest teachers this country ever had) has become a rigid, overpoweringly heavy piece of educational machinery, forbidding to the ordinary, reasonably busy person, and filled with indigestible materials. The Chicago list is overloaded with outdated, thoroughly unreadable scientific classics, and desperately short of just the kind of books that might stimulate an interest in serious reading. Again I say that if you start on the Great Books (Chicago or other) seriously and with a sincere willingness to do some work, you will undoubtedly profit by the experience; but if you expect the reading of *any* list of books to do wonders for you, you'll be disappointed.

And now let's look into the matter a little more deeply. Let's forget about such books as *Silas Marner* or Kant's *Fundamental Principles of the Metaphysic of Morals*. Let's take the *Bible*, *Hamlet*, or Plato's *Dialogues*. Everyone knows that reading these books does something to you. What exactly is it? What are we after when we open one of those books? What is it that makes a classic a classic?

In modern psychological terms, the answer is that it will change your mental set or raise the level of your aspirations and energies. In old-fashioned terms, the answer is that it will elevate your spirit. I prefer these terms: I find it simple and satisfying to define a classic as a book known to elevate the spirit.

And that's why I can't take much stock in the idea of going through a list of books, or "covering" a fixed number of selections, or anyway striving for the blessed state of having read this, that, or the other. Having read a book means nothing. *Reading* a book may be the most tremendous experience of your life; *having read* it is an item in your memory, part of your receding past, a half-forgotten incident of little consequence. You say you have read *King Lear*? What does that mean to you today? How much of it can you quote? How much of it *do* you quote to yourself in situations where such a reminder would help you get on with the job of living?

Why we have that odd faith in the magic of having read a book, I don't know. We don't apply the same principle elsewhere: We don't believe in *having heard* Mendelssohn's violin concerto—we know that it will act on our emotions only while we are listening to it; we don't think that *having seen* the Cathedral of Chartres will unfailingly exert an influence on the remainder of our lives; we don't think that *having climbed* a mountain is more important than climbing it. And yet, we firmly believe in the magic of *having read* a great book.

The whole point of reading the classics becomes clear to you only after you have freed yourself of that superstitious

notion. Forget about the famous books, the lists, the packages
of one hundred Best or one hundred Great. Forget, if you can,
your educationally induced neurosis, your feeling of shame
and guilt at never having read Dante, your unpleasant sensations of not having the faintest notion who Sextus Empiricus
was or being utterly unable to distinguish between *As You
Like It, Twelfth Night,* and *Much Ado About Nothing.* Taste
the delicious feeling of admitting frankly that you never read
a line of a Greek play, a German philosopher, or *any* Italian
author. Don't fall into the opposite error of taking pride in
your ignorance; just look at these matters realistically and be
sincere with the world and with yourself.

And then, when you have gotten rid of all those obsessions
and compulsions—then you can really do something about
your reading. You can draw up your own list of famous books
you have always wanted to read and never did; you can sample
them, drop them if they don't suit you or go on if they do; you
can venture into fields you don't know anything about; you
can read one book fast and the next one very slowly, underlining, making notes and excerpts, memorizing bits and
phrases; you can discover an author you specially like and
read everything he ever wrote; you can discard everything
else and take Marcus Aurelius or Thomas à Kempis wherever
you go; or you can reread the books that are the great classics
of your own life.

Before I started on this chapter, I did just that: I reread
two books that played a great role in my own life. Neither
of them is on any list of classics or great books that I ever
saw; but each has had for me the mysterious magic that makes
a classic.

The first of the two are the letters of Rainer Maria Rilke,

particularly those he wrote when, as a young man in Paris, he served as secretary to the sculptor Auguste Rodin. There is a passage where he sits with Rodin on a park bench and the master answers his question about the meaning of life. *"Il faut travailler,"* Rodin says simply, "one must work." That was Rodin's motto; that was the phrase that stirred me unforgettably when I read the book twenty years ago.

The other book is *The Shadow Line* by Joseph Conrad. Not one of his famous masterpieces; just a simple tale of a young man, almost a boy, who suddenly is named captain of a sailing ship and sets out on a voyage in the Indian Ocean. There is a dead calm that lasts seventeen days, the whole crew gets sick with tropical fever, he discovers that there is no quinine on board—in short, he goes through three weeks of hell. When he lands, he has crossed the shadow line that separates youth from maturity, and he is a man. Conrad doesn't draw any particular moral from this, except for a casual remark by an old sea captain who tells the hero: "A man should stand up to his bad luck, to his mistakes, to his conscience and all that sort of thing. Why—what else would you have to fight against."

I have read innumerable other books in my life, but I think these two helped me most when I was young. Now that I have reread them, I can still understand why—and even recapture my feelings of twenty years ago.

I am not trying to nominate Rilke's letters and Conrad's *Shadow Line* for the list of the world's hundred best books. On the contrary. I told you about them as examples of non-classics that may, for a certain life, do what the classics are supposed to do—elevate the spirit. I say, don't read the classics —try to discover your own classics; every life has its own.

They may be different books at different stages of your life; the same book may produce a tremendous effect one year and fall flat the next; or—what happens more often—a book that left you cold when you read it as a student may change your whole outlook when you pick it up again. Never forget that the world's great books were written by and for grownups; perversely, we read them when we are too young to understand them but neglect them when we have reached the age where they would do us any good.

If you do read great books in that spirit, things may happen to you that you never dreamed of. I told you about my own reading of Rilke and Conrad; but reading can have even more striking results. Let me give you some examples.

Here is a passage from the lecture "A Way of Life" by Sir William Osler, the great physician:

> In the summer of 1871 I was attending the Montreal General Hospital. Much worried as to the future, partly about the final examination, partly as to what I should do afterwards, I picked up a volume of Carlyle, and on the page I opened there was the familiar sentence—"*Our main business is not to see what lies dimly at a distance, but to do what lies clearly at hand.*" A commonplace sentiment enough, but it hit and stuck and helped, and was the starting-point of a habit that has enabled me to utilize to the full the single talent entrusted to me.

Or listen to this, from the autobiography of William Allen White, the famous editor of the *Emporia Gazette*:

> That year the big thing that Vernon Kellogg did for me was to take me across the street from the college into the

second floor of the bank building, where the city library
was housed. The gray-haired librarian, Mrs. Carpenter, let
me loaf there and brought me books. In Eldorado I had
been thrilled by Emerson's line in the essay on *Self-Reliance:* "Trust thyself: every heart vibrates to that iron string."
And I asked Mrs. Carpenter for the essay. It was a snowy
February day when I had just turned seventeen; and as I
read that essay my spirit expanded as though I had heard
the trumpet call of life. I was thrilled and stirred and
literally overturned. I doubt if I have ever been moved so
deeply by anything else that I have read. So I read all the
essays and other Emersonian books and was glad to live
and proud to feel that I was beginning to understand something of the puzzle of life.

Third, here is a bit from the first chapter of *Wake Up and
Live!* by Dorothea Brande, a self-help book that preaches the
gospel of "Act as if it were impossible to fail." This is how
Mrs. Brande hit upon her idea:

Between one minute and the next, I found the idea which
set me free. . . . I was not consciously looking for it; I was
engaged on a piece of research in quite another field. But
I came across a sentence in the book I was reading, *Human
Personality* by F. W. H. Myers, which was so illuminating
that I put the book aside to consider all the ideas suggested
in that one penetrating hypothesis. When I picked up the
book again I was a different person.

Finally, a quotation from the autobiography of the French
writer Romain Rolland, who tells how his life was changed by
reading Spinoza when he was a boy:

One page was enough—the first: four *Definitions* and a few sparks of fire that were struck from the flint of the *Ethics*. I have no illusion about it, nor do I wish others to have any. I do not claim either that the efficacy of that miracle had its source in magic words, nor that I seized Spinoza's true meaning at that time. . . . In Spinoza's text, I discovered, not him, but my unknown self. In the inscription traced over the entrance to the *Ethics*, in those *Definitions* in flaming letters, I read, not what he had said, but what I wanted to say—the words that my own childish thoughts were trying to stutter with my inarticulate tongue. No one ever reads a book. He reads himself through books, either to discover or to control himself. And the most objective books are the most deceptive. The greatest book is not the one whose message engraves itself on the brain, as a telegraphic message on the ticker tape, but the one whose vital impact opens up other viewpoints, and from writer to reader spreads the fire that is fed by the various essences, until it becomes a vast conflagration leaping from forest to forest.

This is what reading can do. This is what reading the Bible has done to millions of deeply religious people; this is what reading Emerson's *Self-Reliance*, Thoreau's *Walden*, Longfellow's *Psalm of Life* has done to thousands of Americans of an earlier generation. Somehow, for many of us, those sources of strength don't have the same power any more. We don't idly open the books of Carlyle any longer, like Sir William Osler, and even if we did, the words wouldn't set our souls on fire.

But great books are still being written. And there are books of previous generations still meaningful to us today; and books overlooked in earlier, more peaceful ages that fit our own turbulent, anxiety-laden century. Let's forget about *Silas Marner*; let's keep up the search for books to live by *today*.

I can think of no better way to conclude this chapter than to add a few quotations—a sort of miniature anthology of passages that have, potentially, the magic I was talking about. These random quotes may not mean anything to you at this moment; but who knows, you may find yourself in the depth of despair at two o'clock in the morning some day, and one of these sentences may give you the courage to keep on living.

So here is Leonardo da Vinci:

Experience is never at fault; it is only our judgment that is in error, in promising itself things that are not within its power. Wrongly do we cry out against experience and with bitter reproaches accuse her of deceitfulness.

Let experience alone and rather turn your complaints against your own ignorance, which causes you to be so carried away by your vain and insensate desires as to expect from experience things which it is not within her power to supply.

Kierkegaard:

It is very dangerous to go into eternity with possibilities which one has oneself prevented from becoming realities. A possibility is a hint from God. One must follow it. In every man there is latent the highest possibility; one must follow it. If God does not wish it, then let him prevent it, but one must not hinder oneself. Trusting to God I have dared, but I was not successful; in that is to be found peace, calm, a confidence in God. I have not dared: that is a woeful thought, a torment in eternity.

Vincent Van Gogh:

I always think that the best way to know God is to love many things. Love a friend, a wife, something, whatever you like, but one must love with a lofty and serious intimate sympathy, with strength, with intelligence, and one must always try to know deeper, better, and more. That leads to God; that leads to unwavering faith.

Samuel Butler:

Happiness and misery consist in progression towards better or worse: it does not matter how high up or low down you are, it depends not on this, but on the direction in which you are tending.

William James:

Fear of life in one form or another is the great thing to exorcise.

Dickens:

Possibly we might even improve the world a little, if we got up early in the morning, and took off our coats to the work.

E. M. Forster:

One must be fond of people and trust them if one is not to make a mess of life.

4
Does Vocabulary-Building Pay?

Let the child's vocabulary, therefore, be limited;
it is very undesirable that he should have more
words than ideas, that he should be able to say
more than he thinks. One of the reasons why
peasants are generally shrewder than townsfolk
is, I think, that their vocabulary is smaller. They
have few ideas, but those few are thoroughly
grasped.

—ROUSSEAU, Emile

AMONG EDUCATIONAL DRUGS AND
prescriptions, vocabulary-building is by far
the newest. "Correct grammar," as we have seen, goes back
to the year 1762 and the venerable Bishop Lowth; the best-
books-package idea started most respectably in 1887 with Sir
John Lubbock's list of one hundred Best Books. The history
of vocabulary-building is considerably shorter and humbler.
It began in 1934 in Hoboken, New Jersey; its begetter was Mr.
Johnson O'Connor, director of something called the Human
Engineering Laboratory.

It seems that during the early thirties Mr. O'Connor, working on something entirely different, began to give vocabulary tests to various occupational groups. Looking over the results, he was seized by the idea that a mysterious relationship between vocabulary size and annual cash income could be statistically shown. He looked again, animated by the same spirit that made Newton look again at the fallen apple. It was true—it was true! The figures spoke for themselves: the vocabulary of well-heeled business executives was larger than that of other mortals, even including poor but presumably erudite college professors.

Mr. O'Connor proudly announced his discovery to the world. In February, 1934, he published an article "Vocabulary and Success" in the *Atlantic Monthly*. "An exact and extensive vocabulary," he wrote on a distinct note of triumph, "is an important concomitant of success. So much is known. Furthermore, such a vocabulary can be acquired. . . . The balance of evidence at the moment suggests that such a consciously, even laboriously achieved vocabulary is an active asset."

And then the rush was on. Vocabulary-building books began to appear in a steady stream. Vocabulary courses started in universities, in colleges, even in high schools. The *Reader's Digest* began a monthly feature called "It Pays to Increase Your Word Power." Full-page ads kept reminding everybody that VOCABULARY LEADS TO QUICK ADVANCEMENT—A HANDFUL OF WORDS WILL CHANGE YOUR LIFE—READ ABOUT THIS NEW VOCABULARY DISCOVERY AND GET THAT RAISE—WORD POWER IS THE KEY TO SUCCESS, POWER AND HAPPINESS. Faith in vocabulary-building got as firmly lodged in our national culture as belief in Mother's Day or the struggle against halitosis. As I write, it has become almost impossible to tell anyone softly and quietly that vocabulary-building is a pointless waste of time and has no practical value whatever. People won't even listen. Vocabulary-building is important because how else can you increase your vocabulary? Everybody knows that a large vocabulary is good for you, don't they? Why *of course* vocabulary-building is good for you—it's like reading the Bible, like eating green leafy vegetables, like saving money for a rainy day. . . .

There is little doubt that vocabulary-building is the greatest educational success story of our times. Nevertheless, I repeat, it is of absolutely no practical value.

But what about the evidence? you say. What about the tests, the experiments, the statistics? What about O'Connor's great discovery? Naturally I asked myself the same question. I decided to find out. I looked at all the ads, all the evidence cited in books, all the relevant material I could possibly find. The astonishing result of my research is this: There has been no published scientific evidence of the supposed connection between vocabulary and success ever since Mr. O'Connor published his original article. The whole "science" of vocabulary-building is based solely and exclusively on those New Jersey tests of 1934. Mr. O'Connor's famous study—which has since been reprinted all over the place some twenty or thirty times—is to this day the only source where a researcher can check the vocabulary-builders' claims that the words they peddle are worth their weight in gold.

Let's see what actually happened in Hoboken twenty years ago. It was this:

There was a vocabulary test, consisting of 150 words. It was given to high school freshmen (average number of errors: 76); to college freshmen (average errors: 42); to college graduates (average errors: 27); and to college professors (average errors: 8). Finally there was a group of seventy-five "major executives"—businessmen who had been presidents or vice presidents of corporations for at least ten years. When these seventy-five men took the test it turned out that their average number of errors was seven—one less than the average of the college teachers. Did those executives build up their vocabulary and *then* climb the ladder of success? Of course not: They took the test *after* they had arrived at the top—and beat the college teachers by one point.

Before we go on, let's play for a moment with those figures. (After all, they are the sum total of scientific evidence for the success-magic of vocabulary-building.) So there were seventy-five executives; let's assume there were also seventy-five college teachers. The executives scored seven errors, the professors eight. What does this difference amount to? If you look closely, you will find that one undereducated college teacher—let's say Mortimer P. Schimpfwort, assistant professor of physical education—could have single-handedly caused that one-point difference: all he needed to do was to make eighty-two errors on the test. I don't mean to say, of course, that this is what actually happened. I do say, however, that the one-point difference between the executives and the professors is practically meaningless. Mr. O'Connor's famous experiment does *not* show that vocabulary is the royal road to financial heights; all it shows is that the vocabulary of middle-aged professionals *or* executives is apt to be higher than that of students. You may have a large vocabulary and make a lot of money; or you may have an equally large vocabulary and spend your life vainly trying to eke out a meager college teacher's salary. On Mr. O'Connor's own evidence, the connection between vocabulary and success doesn't exist.

Even if it did, though, it would be completely irrational to increase your vocabulary deliberately. Suppose the facts were proven: suppose we did know for sure that successful businessmen have a larger vocabulary than the rest of mankind. So what? Does this mean that vocabulary-stuffing will produce vice presidents? No: a big vocabulary is an incidental by-product of an executive's career. As he goes on and up, he learns the words associated with his product, with sales, with management, with legal matters, with personnel work, and with just day-to-day living, talking about lots of things, meeting lots of people, reading lots of letters, and going through the contents of the morning paper every day for some twenty-five or thirty years. Vocabulary comes to him as he gains experience. While worrying about meeting his payroll, he unconsciously adds to his stock of words. Otherwise—if he spent his time on vocabulary-building instead of paying attention to his job—he would soon be out of business and his days as an executive would be over.

The whole upside-down logic of vocabulary-building can be neatly illustrated by the following parallel. Suppose someone makes a study of the relationship between baldness and intelligence. (As a matter of fact, I read something of the sort several years ago. It seems that the incidence of baldness among members of the National Academy of Sciences is considerably higher than among the population as a whole.) Suppose an article is published about that study. The article gets wide attention, the notion spreads around that baldness will make you smarter and thus enable you to earn more money. Pretty soon little bottles appear on drugstore counters variously labeled as "top hair removers," "billiard ball drops" and "anti-locks." Books appear, courses are announced, full-page ads tell the populace about THE WAY TO BALDNESS AND POWER,

HOW TO GET RID OF UNSEEMLY HAIR, THE SHINY ROAD TO SUC-CESS and HOW TO BECOME AN EGGHEAD IN THIRTY DAYS. The years pass, baldness-increasing becomes a respectable, well-established industry and everybody accepts without a murmur the basic premise that baldness leads to success. Is that impossible? Not at all. It happened before our eyes in the field of vocabulary-building.

In the years since Mr. O'Connor's epoch-making discovery, competition in the vocabulary industry has become stiffer and stiffer. There are only so and so many words in the English language that lend themselves to vocabulary-building, and the possible combinations and permutations are soon exhausted. You can give the customers various devices to work new words into their conversation, you can dish the words out at the rate of ten a day or a hundred a week or whatnot, you can throw in bits of grammar, etymology, syntax, literary history, science, or musicology. In the end, however, you will have to meet the competition by offering more and rarer words. That's why the most recent among the fifty or more vocabulary-building texts go in for some of the most outlandish words anybody ever saw.

Here are some of the gems I noted down in my research for this chapter:

Ailurophile means a cat-lover. (You may be able to use this word if you are alert and catch just the right moment.)

Hircine means goatlike. (With this one my imagination fails me.)

Nimiety means excess. (My example: "I ate a nimiety of dessert at lunch.")

A *kibe*, I am sorry to inform you, is a chilblain on the heel. (If you happen to have a chilblain on the heel, it's easy of course to murmur casually "Got a kibe, you know—very painful." If you are not equipped with one, however, the problem is vastly more difficult. "Hurts like a kibe" is the best I can offer, but the solution is far from perfect.)

Then there is *sphygmomanometer*. A sphygmano—, pardon me, a sphygmomanometer is an instrument to measure blood pressure. (Very useful, I am sure, in the medical world, but limited in its possibilities for laymen. Let's try: "I was so mad I could have burst a sphygmomanometer." Not bad; not bad at all. How about this? "You don't happen to have a sphygmomanometer on you by any chance? Left mine at home this morning; had to run for the train." Ah well.)

Finally, you can increase your vocabulary by adding the word *triskaidekaphobia*—fear of the number thirteen. (This one is easy as pie: "Would you like to come over for dinner tonight? My wife has a slight case of triskaidekaphobia, but it's nothing serious.")

Even these beauties don't exhaust the possibilities. A true vocabulary-builder is not fazed by such obstacles as running out of words. He can always make up some new ones for the trade. You don't believe me? I herewith declare, under oath if necessary, that in one of the fifty books I found the word *verborrhea*—plus elaborate instructions on how to add it to your stock of words. Now the word *verborrhea* doesn't exist. The author of that vocabulary book made it up. To be sure, the English language does contain the word *logorrhea*, which Webster defines as "excessive and often incoherent talkativeness." But *verborrhea*, no. It's an ugly monstrosity, made up of a Latin and a Greek root. I checked all the dictionaries and it isn't in any of them. You just have to take my word for it:

that vocabulary-building expert sold his paying customers a word he made up for the purpose.

However, let's forget about such excesses—or "nimieties." The basic issue is this: What's the effect of vocabulary-building? Suppose you go out and buy the advertised educational medicine: what will it do to you?

To answer that question, let me first tell you about a student I once had in one of my writing classes. His first assignment was very poor and contained the following sentence: "The housing situation today is nefarious." Naturally that five-dollar word in his otherwise inexpensively worded paper looked fishy to me. I asked him how come. What did he mean by calling the housing situation nefarious? He smiled in embarrassment and confessed that he had taken a vocabulary-building course in the preceding semester and felt he *had* to use at least one of his precious new words. Maybe he didn't really mean nefarious, he mumbled—showing plainly that he hadn't the faintest notion of the true meaning of the word.

Then there is the more amusing, though possibly apocryphal story of the college girl who wanted to be excused from class before the end of the hour. She had a ten o'clock assignation with her French teacher, she explained. (The dictionary defines *assignation* as an appointment for an illicit love meeting.)

What I mean to say is this: As soon as you have succeeded in adding new words to your vocabulary, you are forever faced by difficult and often embarrassing situations. A larger vocabulary is not an asset but a liability. Like the man who had to sort oranges by size, you are faced with decisions, decisions, decisions all day long. If you *don't* use the new words, you will have wasted the money, time and effort you put into acquiring them, and will doubtless forget them in a short while. If you do use them, you will expose yourself continually to doubts, the fear of mistakes, awkward situations and misunderstandings.

I am not exaggerating. I know from my own experience that what I say is literally true. Let me give you a few examples. (I don't mean to say that I went in for vocabulary-building for the sake of writing this chapter, but I naturally have added many words to my vocabulary in the course of my life and have run into a generous sample of the vocabulary-increaser's problems.)

For instance, the word *viable* is fairly common in scientific and academic writing. It means "capable of living, fit to live" and is used of embryos, young plants, and so forth. It's also a handy word to use in talking about ideas, business schemes, newly founded organizations and such.

I distinctly remember that I used that word once while sitting in my living room and talking to some friends after dinner. They looked at me and didn't understand; in fact, they said so. Naturally I explained the meaning of the word and that was that. However, to me it was a painfully embarrassing incident—so painful that I remember it to this day, after a good many years have gone by. My vocabulary increase had caused me to make my friends and guests feel inferior, by showing them that I casually used words they had never heard about. I cannot remember a single instance where knowledge of the word *viable* proved an advantage in my life; but I do know that on that evening it cost me some tiny fraction of intimacy and friendly feeling.

Or take the word *serendipity*. *Serendipity* is a lovely word. It was coined by Horace Walpole in 1754 from the title of a Persian fairy tale "The Three Princes of Serendip." The three princes "were always making discoveries, by accident or sagacity, of things they were not in quest of." Serendipity is therefore "the faculty of making happy and unexpected discoveries by accident." It's a word that has had a sort of vogue lately and keeps cropping up in all sorts of books and magazines.

I have often tried to use *serendipity* in conversation. The results were not encouraging. Either I realized in the last split second that the word was probably unknown to the person I was talking to, in which case I passed up the chance of using it; or I did use it—and was then forced to explain it, smiling apologetically and trying hard to pretend I had run across it just yesterday. Not once have I been able to use the word freely and to good effect.

Next, let's consider the word *barkable*. I found *barkable* in one of the delightful word-collection books by the British writer Ivor Brown. (Mr. Brown wrote altogether six books on odd and interesting words, published in this country in three double-decker volumes. They are called A *Word in Your Ear*, *I Give You My Word*, and *No Idle Words*. If you love words and don't know the Brown series, get it immediately.) Brown found *barkable* in the following quotation from a thirteenth-century treatise: "It profiteth the lord to have discreet shepherds, watchful and kindly, so that the sheep be not tormented by their wrath but crop their pasture in peace and joyfulness; for it is a token of the shepherd's kindness if the sheep be not scattered abroad but browse around him in company. Let him provide himself with a good barkable dog and lie nightly with his sheep."

I think *barkable* is a charming word. (Brown also has an article on *conversible*, which is constructed the same way. He quotes Jane Austen: "The evening was quiet and conversible.") Ever since I came across *barkable*, I have planned to use it. Nothing easier: we have a large dog; people ask perennially "Does he bite?" Why can't I answer pleasantly: "No, he doesn't bite—he's just barkable"? Why can't I? I don't know.

Then there is *dacoity*. One nice day I was reading an editorial in the *New York Times* and came upon the following: "The very fragmentation of the country, the brigandage or dacoity, the bewildering array of political parties that include at least two warring varieties of Communists, the lack of communications, all serve to create a vortex instead of the vacuum that the Communists like." What was meant by *dacoity*? I had never seen or heard the word before. I went to the dictionary and found: "Gang robbery in India and Burma." That wasn't too helpful since the editorial dealt with Burma and so the dictionary didn't tell me anything I hadn't already guessed. But at any rate, my vocabulary had been enriched by a beautifully melodious word—musical, strong-sounding, vaguely menacing. I am determined to use it at the next opportunity but must confess that so far conversation around me has never veered toward Burma. As soon as it does, I'll be ready with "And don't forget all the horrible dacoity that's going on over there."

Meanwhile I have found a splendid solution. *Dacoity* seems to be made for use as a personal swearword. It sounds good, it has a ring of violence about it, and it's got rhythm. I have added it to my repertory and shall use it on special occasions. "Hell and dacoity!" I am sure it will provide excellent emotional relief.

Now I come to the humble word *zwieback*. Nothing very wonderful about *zwieback*; it doesn't compare with *dacoity* or *serendipity.* You probably know what a zwieback is; it's a sort of dry, hard toast or bread. I have known the word *zwieback* ever since I can remember: it is German and German is my native language. The trouble is this, however: the proper German pronunciation is *tsveeback* or, if you want to Anglicize it a little, *tsweeback.* This is the pronunciation that's listed first in all the dictionaries. It is not what people say, though. The people—every single person I ever heard pronounce the word —say *swyeback.*

Before I learned about the dangers of vocabulary-building, I naturally pronounced *zwieback* the way it is supposed to be pronounced, namely, *tsweeback.* I was finally cured of the habit when I tried to order zwieback in a restaurant and got nothing but an empty stare. Moral: Words gained by "book l'arning" won't do you any good.

Or let's take *vastidities.* I came across *vastidities* in a *New Yorker* profile of Roland Butler, the publicity director of the Ringling Brothers and Barnum & Bailey Circus. Mr. Butler is being paid for saying and writing things like this: "Twenty-six displays with scores of acts. Funambulists (wire walkers) with unparalleled terpsichorean gyrations that beggar description; proboscidean mammals (that is, elephants) in the most amazing display of pachydermic skill the world has ever known." He once told a reporter: "In New York, we claimed our show was so big that it overflowed the 'vastidities' of Madison Square Garden. 'Vastidities' is in the dictionary too, but I think that was going a little too far. You can use words like that to the point at which it gets a little sickening, don't you know." Possibly, but I still would like to use *vastidities* at least once, just to see what it feels like.

Or *frangipani.* In *Delight,* a book of essays by J. B. Priestley, he talks about how he was approaching Tahiti one time and about the delight the smell gave him. "It was compounded of copra, decayed fish, frangipani and vanilla, oil and sweat, stew and fries, dung and blossom." I knew all the ingredients except frangipani, and got a kick out of finding that it is red jasmine perfume. The problem, again, is how to use the word naturally in conversation. There is too little red jasmine perfume in our lives to talk about.

Finally, my darling among all the words in the dictionary: *cicisbeo*. A cicisbeo, in eighteenth-century Italy, was the "recognized gallant or *cavalier servente* of a married woman." For a century or so, cicisbeism was a flourishing social institution.

What do you do with *cicisbeo* once you have added the word to your vocabulary? (It's pronounced *cheecheezbay-o*, by the way.) I have known the word for many years now, but I have never even approached a solution of the problem. "Darling, let me be your cicisbeo"? Obviously unsuitable. "I used to be a cicisbeo during the depression"? No good. "Met George on the train this morning—you know, he was Clara's cicisbeo last summer"? I wonder. I'm afraid the investment in *cicisbeo* was a total loss.

Seriously, though—— Seriously, though, I find it impossible to be serious about vocabulary-building. And for a very good reason: vocabulary-building is one of mankind's best sources of unconscious humor. Increase your vocabulary and sooner or later you'll make yourself utterly ridiculous.

Let me show you why this is so. What kind of words do you add to your vocabulary when you try to increase it? Obviously words you don't know and don't ordinarily use. Now—considering the fact that without vocabulary-building you have

been able to get along perfectly, never condemned to speech-
lessness because you couldn't find the word to express what
you wanted to say—considering the plain fact, I say, that
your present vocabulary has served you faithfully so far in all
circumstances and contingencies—the words you add will
necessarily be extra words, words on the fringe of your life,
words that *may* be used for the things you are talking about
but don't have to. Where do you find words like that? You
find them in two possible places:

First, words that belong to a certain special field and aren't
ordinarily used outside it—words like *viable* (which comes
from biology) or *dacoity* (which comes from Burma).

Second, words that are found in print but aren't ordinarily
used in speaking—words like *barkable, vastidities,* or *cicisbeo.*

Now both kinds of words are not meant to be used outside
their natural habitat. You can't use *dacoity* unless you talk
about Burma or India and you can't use *cicisbeo* unless you talk
about eighteenth-century Italy. You can't use *viable, barkable,*
or *vastidities* unless you use them naturally talking about the
kinds of subjects that lend themselves to being discussed in
those terms. If you leave such words in the contexts where they
belong, they will sound all right, but if you pull them out and
transplant them, they will play you tricks. You can refer to
"the vastidities of Madison Square Garden," but people will
think you are going too far. You can call your dog a barkable
dog, but people will think you are talking funny English. You
can use *viable* in conversation, but you are apt to lose friends
and alienate people.

And so, for these excellent reasons, the words that are
packaged and merchandised by the vocabulary-builders are
hardly ever used by the people who already know them. They

save them up for a special purpose: they use them strictly for laughs.

About two years ago I did some research on the word usage of a group of eminent people in various fields. I soon realized that I had a special problem on my hands when it came to words like *egress, sylvan, aver, well nigh, stentorian, repast,* or *peradventure.* Each member of the test group knew these words but not one of them admitted to using them except for humorous purposes. Such words, they felt, belonged in a special compartment of their vocabulary—they were something like Christmas decorations or trick gadgets for parties.

Rare, unusual words are in fact the stock in trade of a certain type of humorist. The type was more common fifty or a hundred years ago, but it is still flourishing. Perhaps the best practitioner in America today is S. J. Perelman. Here's an example:

"With barely potable spirits fetching a king's ransom these days, and the price of barbiturates indistinguishable from that of gold dust, it ought to interest anyone looking for a little fast surcease that the best fifteen-cent nepenthe in town is still Louella Parsons' monthly column in *Modern Screen.*"

You see how the incomparable Mr. Perelman does it? *Potable, surcease, nepenthe* . . . they are all words dearly beloved by vocabulary teachers and students, to be taken up only at an advanced stage of higher word-learning. Happy the day when the fifteen-minutes-a-day scholar learns that you can say *potable* for something you can drink, *surcease* instead of *relief,* and *nepenthe* for *sedative!* He studies the new words, he memorizes them, he drills them and hammers them into his mind—and finally he uses them. And the effect? Unconscious, watered-down S. J. Perelman.

You probably think that I exaggerate, that the vocabulary experts know better than giving their customers words that will embarrass them and make them sound like fools. But here is the evidence:

Take the most widely used vocabulary-building book and look up the word *bivalve*. You will find that the student is urged to learn its meaning and add it to his vocabulary. Then look up the same word in Fowler's *Modern English Usage*. There you will find "the succulent bivalve" listed under the heading *Pedantic and Polysyllabic Humour*. Says Fowler: "The playful use of long or learned words is a one-sided game boring the reader more than it pleases the writer . . . Yielding to the impulse is a confession of failure."

Or take *animadvert*, a word solemnly taught to the readers of the same widely used vocabulary book. Then listen to Ivor Brown in *No Idle Words*: "An odd and foolish verb. 'Do you animadvert on me, Sir?' is not common conversational English, but indignant letter-writers in the Press do frequently allude to those who animadvert on this cause or that person."

Next, turn to *bête noire*, number one of a list of fifteen "challenging" words in the same famous vocabulary book. "The above words," says the book,

> are extremely valuable to anyone, but on the whole they are quite difficult and their meanings are known to comparatively few. The following exercise will help fix the unfamiliar ones in the mind of the reader. Several of the words are repeated. . . .

Bête noire is repeated, you can be sure. And what has the reader got when he has fixed that challenging, extremely valuable word in his mind? For the answer I refer you to Eric Partridge's *Dictionary of Clichés*. You will find *bête noire* listed there with an asterisk. The asterisk means that it is "a particularly hackneyed or objectionable cliché." And what is a cliché? A cliché is, in Mr. Partridge's excellent definition, "a phrase, or short sentence, that has become so hackneyed that careful speakers and scrupulous writers shrink from it."

Pedantic and polysyllabic humor, clichés, misused technical terms, faintly amusing archaisms, out-of-date slang, stale metaphors, irrelevant allusions, foreign words apt to be misspelled, mispronounced or misapplied—that's what the vocabulary-builders have to offer, that's what is sold for cash to hundreds of thousands eager to improve their English. I repeat, this is not an exaggeration but the simple truth.

We all have, by necessity, the vocabulary that corresponds to our life, our background, our accumulated experience. In the normal course of affairs that vocabulary grows: we get around, we learn new things, we meet new people, we soak up words from what we hear and read. This *grown* vocabulary consists of good, useful words, words we know what to do with, words that fit.

As soon as we try to increase our vocabulary artificially, we disturb our normal linguistic balance. We stuff our brains with words that don't come naturally—"boughten" words —store words. And those store words never fit.

Yes, it is a sad, inexorable law of language and nature that *built vocabulary never fits*. There is no redeeming feature of vocabulary-building. True, all efforts toward self-improvement will make you feel good; but otherwise, I am sorry to say, vocabulary-building won't get you anywhere and may even lead to painful social lapses.

No redeeming feature, did I say? Pardon me, I forgot to mention one very important aspect of this whole business: vocabulary-building may raise your I.Q. Not really, of course, but since vocabulary questions are part of all intelligence tests, vocabulary-building will make you *look* smarter than you are when you take a test.

In fact, I strongly suspect that the real father of the whole vocabulary movement was not the ingenious Mr. O'Connor but some unknown bright twelve- or fourteen-year-old who first saw that it is possible to cram for an intelligence test. To the testers, vocabulary was of course a splendidly measurable *symptom* of intelligence; they did not foresee that sooner or later youngsters would learn to fake the symptom. But they did; they did indeed; they infected the whole country with the perverse idea that you can improve your mind by memorizing a lot of words.

And so, when you get down to it, vocabulary-building is a sort of intellectual makeup or mental false teeth. You don't really care for that, do you?

5

Specify!

*His substance also was seven thousand sheep,
and three thousand camels, and five hundred
yoke of oxen, and five hundred she asses, and a
very great household; so that this man was the
greatest of all the men of the east.*

—Job, 1:3

YOU HAVE JUST READ THREE CHAPTERS HEADED by questions. I expressed, in so many words, my doubts about certain popular methods of improving your speech and writing. I told you that I don't take much stock in "correct grammar," that I consider the "One Hundred Best Books" idea a delusion, that vocabulary-building seems to me rather ridiculous. I realize that it's high time I offered you something positive. All right, here it is. This chapter is headed "Specify!"—with an exclamation point. "Specify!" is the most important rule to follow in all your communication.

What do I mean by "Specify!"? Just this: Learn to be specific; concentrate on details; give names, dates, places, facts, and figures; focus on the visible, audible, measurable; pass on your direct experience—rather than your thoughts, opinions, general ideas.

Old stuff, you say. A platitude. The Five W's—who, what, when, where, why—everybody has heard about that. Everybody does it naturally, without thinking.

But there you are wrong. The rule of being specific is *not* as old as speaking and writing. On the contrary, the idea is fairly new. It's a recent development of modern civilization.

Look at it this way. Speaking, reading, writing—the use of words—used to be an *incidental* part of people's lives. It wasn't what a great many people did for a living. But since the invention of printing and since the development of newspapers the situation has changed. Now there is a large group of people who are paid for putting things in words; we employ the services of thousands and thousands of reporters, feature writers, novelists and short story writers, advertising copywriters, radio and television broadcasters, press agents, and so forth. By far the largest group among these professionals are the reporters.

Now the reporters—the people who practice communication for a living—naturally have worked out some basic principles of their craft. There is a body of knowledge—or a bag of tricks if you will—that is passed on from masters to apprentices. There are established rules of what to do and how to do it. And the main rule—the essence of a reporter's skill—is the rule of the Five W's, the categorical imperative to specify.

Ask a seasoned reporter what he thinks of correct grammar and usage. He'll tell you that he hasn't given it much thought since he started to work for a living. Ask him whether he reads the classics: he won't see much connection between reading books and his job. Ask him how about vocabulary-building; he'll laugh in your face. But ask him about the rule of who, what, when, where, and why, and he'll admit that he uses it every day as automatically and unconsciously as his typewriter. Being a reporter without being specific is impossible.

This hasn't always been so. Fifty or a hundred years ago—even thirty years ago—reporters wrote flowery prose, embellishing their facts with choice adjectives, interlarding their stories freely with their own opinions, observations, and random thoughts. They strove for beautiful writing, thoughtful phrasing, words rather than facts. Even today, this is still true in most parts of the globe. Lean, factual reporting is something that has developed only recently—and mainly in the United States.

Several years ago I lectured to a group of German editors who came here to study American newspaper methods. Most of those men worked on papers that were under the supervision of the American occupational authorities. They found many of our ways of doing things strange and rather hard to learn. The greatest hurdle, however, was our technique of reporting: they simply didn't feel the American newspaperman's ingrained disgust for editorializing the news. To us it may be as natural as breathing that opinions belong on the editorial page and nowhere else; to them it was a novel idea. As far as writing technique goes, they were about half a century behind.

You may argue that these are just two different ways of handling a job, that the European method is just as good as ours, that it's nonsense to talk about progress in such a thing as writing. But I disagree. In fact, I am deeply convinced that the tendency to specify, the respect for facts is exactly the thing that makes for progress in all fields.

Look at science. I suppose you'll admit there has been progress in science. What is the source of that progress? Obviously the application of the scientific method. As A. N. Whitehead wrote, "the greatest invention of the past century was the invention of invention itself." The vast bulk of scientific discoveries today is made by the patient use of the scientific method—in other words, by collecting facts and figures, by close observation, by peering through microscopes, by assembling statistical data. What is it that one generation of scientists passes on to the next? Not the gift of intuition, the ability to form hypotheses, the theoretical framework. Rather, the great rule of being specific, of looking for facts, of doing field work, of checking measurements.

Or take police work. Do you read mystery stories? Then you know in what direction progress in police work has been going. We don't expect any more that the murderer will be caught by sheer brain power on the part of the detective; it's a pleasant miracle to read about, but we know things don't happen that way any more. Criminals are caught today by taking fingerprints, by investigating specks of dust, by comparing the thickness of downstrokes in handwriting, by analyzing the dregs in a coffee cup, by tracing laundry marks on the victim's underwear. In this age, justice is done by paying attention to small details.

The same in the courtroom. A witness, like a modern reporter, is supposed to stick to the Five W's and not to editorialize. Whenever he says "He looked dangerous," counsel for the defense pops up and says "I object. This is the witness's opinion, not an observation." When the witness says

"Everybody knew he was a gangster," he is told that this is hearsay evidence and not admissible. When he says "He told me he was going to kill her," he is promptly asked "What were the defendant's exact words?"

And so it goes. Science, police work, courtroom procedure are all examples of techniques for finding the truth. During the past three or four centuries we have worked out a way to do that. There may be other ways of finding the truth, but this is the one we have learned to rely on; this is what we accept; this is what has become second nature to us. To find the truth, we automatically start by finding the facts.

Exactly the same thing has happened in the field of communication. We have gradually discovered that "Specify!" is the best rule not only for finding the truth but also for telling it. Through the practical experience of professional writers and reporters, we have found that to communicate effectively, we must communicate specific facts. As far as there is *any* scientific method of writing, this is it: give details; quote facts and figures; mention dates and places; repeat exactly what was said; spell the names right.

We are all so used to reporting by this method that we don't notice any more how it's done when we read it in the daily paper. To remind you, I shall quote an example. Here is a news report in the classic style from the front page of the *New York Times*:

CAMBRIDGE, Mass., June 1 [1953]—Dr. Nathan Marsh Pusey, president of Lawrence College in Appleton, Wis., was elected the twenty-fourth president of Harvard by the Harvard Corporation today.

Dr. Pusey, who is a native of Council Buffs, Iowa, and

46 years old, is a scholar in Greek history, and holds three
degrees from Harvard: Bachelor of Arts, magna cum laude,
1928; Master of Arts, 1932, and Doctor of Philosophy,
1937. He prepared for college at Abraham Lincoln High
School in Council Bluffs.

The Iowa educator will succeed Dr. James Bryant
Conant who will become president-emeritus of Harvard
University on Sept. 1. Dr. Conant, now on leave, is serving
as United States High Commissioner for Germany.

Dr. Pusey's election by the Harvard Corporation is subject to the confirmation of the Board of Overseers. This
confirmation, customarily a formality, is scheduled to be
voted on June 10, the day before the Harvard commencement. On only one occasion, in 1868, have the overseers
refused the corporation permission to elect a president.

The occasion of the only refusal was in the election of
Dr. Charles W. Eliot, the original choice of the corporation, as the twenty-first president. The corporation pre-
vailed after a delay of six months, and Dr. Eliot became
president in 1869.

Dr. Pusey, reached by telephone in Appleton, said that
although he considered the corporation's action "a tremendous honor," he declined further comment until after
the meeting of the overseers. . . . [etc. etc.]

Look closely at these eleven sentences and you'll find that
almost every word in them refers to a specific fact. We get
Dr. Pusey's full middle name, the high school he went to,
the reason for Dr. Conant's resignation, the one exception
to the rule that the overseers always confirm the corporation's
choice, and exactly what happened at that occasion. We get

dozens of other specific details. We don't get, however—and don't expect to get—any information about the reporter's own feelings, whether the news makes him happy or unhappy, whether he prefers a historian to a chemist as the president of Harvard, or whether he personally expects Dr. Pusey's election to be confirmed.

Now I ask you to imagine the following. Suppose you have just read this item in the paper and want to convey the information to someone else who doesn't know it. How are you going to do it? Are you going to apply automatically the rule of the Five W's? Are you going to refrain from editorializing? Are you going to perform this little job of communication according to the best professional standards of today? Let's hear you try:

"I see where they picked a new president for Harvard last night. Fellow by name of Percy or Munsey or something—never heard of him, have *you*? Fairly young, forty-something. He's now out in the Middle West someplace—president of a small college in Minnesota—no, Nebraska—no, Wisconsin. The *Times* says he's *got* the nomination but there's some other formality, so it's not really official. *Practically* official, though, the *Times* says . . . Guess Munsey must have been surprised—wonder what went on there behind the scenes. Funny they went all the way to Wisconsin to pick the guy. What field? Oh, didn't I say? He's a Latin teacher."

No, you wouldn't do too well with the assignment—even if your performance were far superior to what I imagined here. You would certainly not give all the relevant facts, you would forget things and mix them up, you would insert some ideas of your own—in other words, you would be sure to make a certain degree of hash of the story.

Of course you are not a reporter. I know. You tell me that you don't plan to compete with the news-writing technique used by the *New York Times*; in casual conversation all that's necessary is to give the general idea. So you may forget most of the details and make minor mistakes about some others —so what? You have managed to communicate the story, and that's what counts.

Or is it? Look again at the two versions and see what happened in the process of transmitting the story from the *Times* by way of your mind to your friend. Not only have you left out scores of details; not only have you changed or blurred some of the facts—but you have also managed to convey some impressions that may be wrong. Maybe Dr. Pusey isn't such a nobody as you indicate; maybe he is famous in academic circles for his work; maybe Lawrence College has an extraordinarily high national standing among colleges. The *Times* reporter left the way open for such impressions; you closed it. Trying to communicate a piece of information you did what most people do: you passed on some facts, some semifacts, and some out-and-out lies.

Whereupon you reluctantly admit that the rule of the Five W's *may* apply to information or straight news. But, you say, it doesn't apply to everything. What about conveying emotions, ideas, theories, flights of fancy? You can't communicate everything by giving names, dates, and percentage figures, can you?

And yet, that's exactly what modern professional writers are trying to do. The rule of "Specify!" has gotten into their blood. Whether they are trained as reporters or not, they are almost universally agreed on writing about anything by giving their readers concrete, specific facts.

This literary method—the method of conveying feelings and ideas by telling facts—has a long history. It can be traced back to fairy tales and heroic epics, to Homer and Tacitus. However, as a modern movement, it is about a hundred years old. The first consistent user of the method was the great French writer Guy de Maupassant. Here is a typical Maupassant passage—the opening paragraphs of his famous short story "A Piece of String":

Along all the roads around Goderville the peasants and their wives were coming towards the little town, for it was market day. The men walked with plodding steps, their bodies bent forward at each thrust of their long bowed legs. They were deformed by hard work, by the pull of the heavy plough which raises the left shoulder and twists the torso, by the reaping of the wheat which forces the knees apart to get a firm stand, by all the slow and strenuous labors of life on the farm. Their blue smocks, starched, shining as if varnished, ornamented with a little design in white at the neck and wrists, puffed about their bony bodies, seemed like balloons ready to carry them off. From each smock a head, two arms, and two feet protruded.

Some led a cow or a calf at the end of a rope, and their wives, walking behind the animal, whipped its haunches with a leafy branch to hasten its progress. They carried on their arms large wicker-baskets, out of which here a chicken and there a duck thrust forth its head. The women walked with a quicker, livelier step than their husbands. Their spare, straight figures were wrapped in a scanty little shawl, pinned over their flat bosoms, and their heads were enveloped in a piece of white linen tightly pressed on the hair and surmounted by a cap.

The passage conveys strong emotion, rising from Maupassant's intimate knowledge of the lives of Norman peasants. And yet, there is not a word betraying these emotions directly. He describes; he writes about spread knees, little white designs, and baskets of chickens. The reader is made to feel whatever the things described will suggest to him.

In our day the most famous practitioner of the method is Ernest Hemingway. Here are, for example, two brief paragraphs from "The Killers." In this story two men enter a lunchroom and sit down at the counter. Later the reader finds out they are hired murderers:

> "I'll take ham and eggs," the man called Al said. He wore a derby hat and a black overcoat buttoned across the chest. His face was small and white and he had tight lips. He wore a silk muffler and gloves.
>
> "Give me bacon and eggs," said the other man. He was about the same size as Al. Their faces were different, but they were dressed like twins. Both wore overcoats too tight for them. They sat leaning forward, their elbows on the counter.

I could fill this book with other examples. They can be found everywhere—in fiction and nonfiction, in drama and poetry. The principle, as I said, is as universal in today's professional writing as observation and experiment are in today's science. A modern scientist is a man forever in search of specific facts; a modern writer is a man forever in search of concrete details.

It's this basic attitude, this yearning for concreteness, this lifelong itch to get down to facts, cases, people, things, colors, sensations, sounds, events, scenes, movement, dialogue, that makes a professional writer what he is. He can't understand other people who don't have that itch. When he gets a letter in the mail, he wants to rewrite it, translating from the abstract to the concrete. When he hears and sees the millions of high flown generalities that fill the world's air and cover the world's paper, he wants to talk back, to ask for practical illustrations, living examples, who-said-exactly-what-to-whom and how-does-this-affect-Mrs.-McNulty-in-Hackensack-New-Jersey. He knows that this is the right way to communicate with other human beings and is disgusted with the tremendous mass of ineffective, useless words that are uttered every day.

The ordinary person never understands this. He thinks the secret of writing is something entirely different. He wants rules—where to put the commas and periods, what words to use, how to make an outline. He wants to know how to handle the English language better—he'll do the rest and supply the material, the ideas to be expressed. Unfortunately things don't work that way: to write well, you must think differently, you must have the itch for reality—for people, things, bicycles, sailing ships, beer mugs, Diesel engines, dolls, marbles, squirrels, and women's hats.

In other words, you must be something of a poet. For poetry, among other things, means the continual translation of feelings and ideas into concrete imagery. In poetry, it is impossible to talk about "families in the middle-income brackets" or "low-calorie, vitamin-rich foods." The reader or listener must be made to see and hear—and touch and smell, if possible. If he can't be made to get the feeling of the thing itself, it's the business of the poet to suggest something that feels *like* it. And so poetry is the source of all similes and metaphors. On looking into Chapman's Homer, the poet is reminded—and reminds the reader—of stout Cortez, silent upon a peak in Darien. Or, to take an equally extraordinary example from the German poet Christian Morgenstern, the poet sees that *"die Möwen sehen alle aus, als ob sie Emma hiessen"*—which means "seagulls all look as if their name was Emma."

Poets, the makers of metaphors, are the makers of language. Or rather, the language-making process is essentially poetry. Some unknown poet once looked at a tall building and first thought of calling it a skyscraper; some other poet, in a less happy moment of his life, found himself in a subway train and gave the language the simile—or cliché—of conditions inside a can of sardines. And way, way back innumerable poets were at work fashioning all the words we have for abstractions and intangibles, comparing their essential ideas with visible, tangible things and events. *Comprehension* once meant "getting a grip on," *education* once meant "drawing out," *recollection* once meant "gathering up." There isn't a word in the English language—or in any other language—that wasn't once a live and kicking image of some thing in the world around us. Language, as has often been said, is a heap of dead metaphors. The poet—and the professional writer in general—feels this and knows it's his job to revive and rejuvenate the language.

Actually, of course, it is everybody's job. We all use our language day in day out, and we are all called upon to be poets, professional writers, or at least good reporters in whatever we say or write. We can't leave the itch for reality, the hunt for details, the image-making process to a few paid specialists. It's up to us. It's up to us to face our responsibilities toward our language.

This is not just a high-sounding phrase. It's a practical

matter. Nothing will improve your speech and writing as much as just that. Try to adopt a professional writer's or reporter's attitude in your thinking, speaking, and writing, and it will do wonders for you.

In your business letters, stop gluing together the same old conventional phrases and words. Be specific. Don't talk about "the management" or "the employees"; use their names—even first names. Remind yourself that your company isn't an abstract economic structure of operations and relationships, but people working at specific hours at specific places, doing specific things with specific materials. Then remind yourself—which is a little harder—that your addressee's company isn't an abstract entity either but also filled with people who have first names, homes, families, cars, financial troubles, and hate to get up in the morning. Once you get the feel of this simple truth, your business correspondence may start resembling the communication of one human being with another.

The same in your private letters. Don't be general; don't write: "Nothing much has been happening here. We are all fine." Be specific. Tell about the last party or what your little girl said last Tuesday.

Apply the same principle in the hardest of all letters—the letter of sympathy. Don't use the old stock phrases. Remember something specific—your last meeting with the person who died, or something about him or her you specially liked. (Which reminds me of the famous Jewish story of the funeral oration. The deceased had been universally despised and the speaker couldn't think of a single good thing to say about him. Finally he said, with tremulous remembrance: "Bagels he liked to eat.")

Adopt the reporter's attitude in your speeches. That doesn't mean that all your speeches should start with a story about Pat and Mike; but they ought to contain stories, illustrations, individual case histories, applications in specific instances, translations of all generalities into concrete terms. Names, dates, places—who, what, when, where, why—tell your audience what you see before your mind's eye.

When you have to write instructions, write them the same way. Don't be general; spell out each step. Here again, good communication is based on the same principle as good science: think "operationally"; analyze the sequence of steps. Visualize what happens first, second, and third, and then tell it, still visually.

Instead of lumping together groups, focus on individuals. Find the typical man and talk about him—mentioning his last name, his first name, if possible even his nickname. (Want to go further? Give the exact address, with street and house number. In Dale Carnegie's *How to Stop Worrying and Start Living* the famous master of popularization does exactly that whenever he mentions one of his readers or correspondents. The effect is remarkable.)

When you describe the history of something, don't pass the years by in review, one neatly following the other, each containing 365 days and an exactly equal amount of events. Pick out the high spots. Look for turning points. Act like a reporter. Focus on the drama and kiss off lightly the drab, dull years in between.

Or do you have to write rules and regulations? If so, I pity you. A rule is by definition general: it resists being made specific. A rule must refer to taxpayers in general rather than Mr. Nettleton or Mrs. Hazeltine; it must say "policyholders" instead of Mr. and Mrs. Mottleback. And yet, you must specify if you want to communicate meaning. You can't expect anyone to read and understand you if you say something like this: "If the named insured is an individual who owns the automobile classified as 'pleasure and business' or husband and wife either or both of whom own said automobile, such insurance as is offered by this policy with respect to said automobile applies with respect to any other automobile, subject to the following provisions. . . ." If you adopt a professional writer's attitude, you have to sit down and work out how this applies to specific human beings in specific situations, and if it takes five pages to explain it, you have to write five pages.

In short, try to stay away from generalities in all your speaking and writing—or, if you *have* to use them, translate them immediately into concrete, specific facts and illustrations. This is difficult and even impossible to carry through, I know. It's particularly hard if you are living and working in an environment that is full of generalities—if you are an executive, a community leader, a social scientist, a speaker or writer on public affairs. Nevertheless, you must forever try. If you are a teacher, go on a strict word diet, rigidly abstaining from such stomach-turning mental fare as "learnings" and "understandings" (in the educational plural) or "peer relationships" (meaning relations between boys and girls of the same age). If you are a social scientist, do penance of twenty-four hours of self-imposed silence whenever you say or write something like "Propinquity continues to foster solidarity, resisting the centrifugal effects of urbanization." (I quote verbatim from a book on sociology I opened at random.) And if you are just an ordinary living-room debater on public affairs, go and stand in a corner whenever you use words like "environmental factors," "social values," or "dynamics." (Maybe, while you are standing there, you will realize that you really didn't mean *anything* when you used those words. Good; go and sin no more.)

Why is this so hard? Why can't we all just make up our minds to abandon all generalities and live happily ever after? Why do we need all these perennial reminders of something everybody feels and knows? What's holding us back from always making sense?

The answer is, Ourselves. We don't talk in concrete, specific terms because of our characters, our personalities, our lifelong habits, our whole mental makeup. If we could learn to "specify" by simply reading about that basic rule in a book and then applying it for the rest of our lives, there would be no problem. We would all speak and write like that automatically, having spent one evening in acquiring a simple trick.

Actually, of course, concreteness isn't something you sprinkle on your words like Parmesan cheese. It's internal: it depends on who you are and what kind of life you live. Or rather, what kind of life you *have* lived so that you are equipped with specific instances and concrete images whenever you need them.

For if you think about it for a moment, you will see that the secret of the modern reporter's and professional writer's style lies not in what he does when he writes. A news report is well written because of what the reporter did *before* he sat down at his typewriter. It's the amount and quality of the legwork that counts. He's been out watching the event, or talking to people, taking down their words, copying figures and data and facts, talking over the telephone, rounding up sources, filling his notebook with material. He is concrete and specific because he's worked up stuff to be concrete and specific *with*.

The same applies to communication in general. Concreteness depends on having had concrete experience. And since ordinary people don't take notes of everything they see and hear, it all depends on perception and memory. We can apply the rule of "Specify!" to the degree that we perceive and remember what goes on around us.

And there is the problem. For we all differ tremendously in our capacities to perceive and remember. In fact, psychologists today consider differences in perception as the key to our whole personality.

Have you ever seen how a Rorschach test works? The Rorschach test is probably the most famous among all personality tests today. It's one of many "projective" tests, that is, tests that analyze personality as projected by its perception of the world around it. They work on the principle that a person is what he sees.

In the Rorschach test you are asked to look at a series of inkblots in jagged and fantastic shapes and tell the tester what you see. Looking at one of the cards, you may see a benign Santa Claus, a couple of dancing elephants, and an old lady sitting under a lamp. Someone else, looking at the same card, may discover a couple of waiters, bowing and swishing their aprons, a clump of tulips, and a map of Africa. Who is right? Nobody of course. But the projected personalities are obviously entirely different.

What has all this to do with writing and speaking and the use of words? More than you think. For your expression in words is just as much a projection of your personality as your perception of figures and animals in an inkblot. In fact, psychologists have made some fascinating studies of the relationship between the two. One of the main differences in personality that a Rorschach test shows, for instance, is the difference between introverts and extraverts—between the person who shies away from reality and the person who welcomes it with open arms. The introvert—the worrying type —will see clouds in the Rorschach inkblots and his analytical mind will look *into* the inklots and discover pictures in depth and perspective. The extravert will see no clouds on the inkblot horizon and will tend to see his pictures flat.

Now the same introvert who sees the world analytically, in perspective, will use words qualitatively and with a tendency to abstraction. His "adjective-verb quotient" will be high. Which means that he will use more adjectives to qualify and generalize and fewer verbs to refer to happenings and events. The extravert, on the other hand, will talk about the world not in static generalities but in dynamic verbs.

Or let's take another widely used projective test, the Thematic Apperception Test (T.A.T.). Here you are asked to look at a series of pictures and tell stories about them. On one picture, for example, there is a scene which might be interpreted as a stabbing or as a surgical operation. What does it mean to you? The answer will serve as a key to your personality. On another picture you see, not quite clearly, an object that may be a revolver. Or it is a fan? Or something else? It's up to you to perceive it in your own terms.

See what I am driving at? You will be specific in your speech and writing depending on how you have perceived things and events in your life. Some people taking a Rorschach test see very little in those inkblots; when they take the T.A.T., they tell brief, meager stories. Their powers of perception are small. They can't communicate much specific detail, like a reporter who has been lazy in doing his legwork. Some others are introverts, peering fixedly at one particular area and paying little attention to the variety of things that go on elsewhere. They will be boring their fellow men with their single-minded concentration and their lack of pleasant small talk. Your perception determines the quality of your speech; and your perception depends on your personality.

But, you say, am I not defeating my own argument? If good speech and writing ultimately depend on perception and personality, then poor communication has to be treated like any other personality trouble—by some kind of medical therapy, perhaps. Do we have to go to a psychiatrist if we want to improve our English?

No. But consider the fact that the habit of close, exact observation is a sort of occupational therapy anyway. I can well imagine a young introvert, shy, afraid of people, worrying about life, who may be cured of those personality troubles by taking on a job as a reporter. There he'll have to go out and talk to people, be on the spot to watch fires and catastrophes, interview the victims of accidents or their widows, talk to important people and to nobodies, get a daily walloping dose of crude life experience whether he likes it or not. Pretty soon his personality will have changed. Training in perception and communication will have made him over.

The same goes for any other kind of professional writer. Look at all the handbooks on writing, the courses in creative self-expression. A single theme runs through them all: Learn to observe, open yourself to experience. Gather material day and night, walking and sleeping (dreams are valuable experience too), eating and working. Keep a notebook handy; use your mind as a camera and file away everything you see. Start by writing about things you are familiar with; and when you are through with that, go out and familiarize yourself with more things, or your writing will come to a dead stop.

And so—and so the great basic rule of "Specify!" still stands. It will help you in all your ordinary tasks of communication by reminding you of the necessity to be concrete. It will nudge you to mention names, dates, and places, to talk about people, things, and events, to be exact, to spell out details, to use pictures, images, cases, illustrations. It will stimulate you to enrich all your talk and your writing by digging down into your direct personal experience, telling stories you have heard, describing events you have witnessed, quoting people you have met, sharing experiences you have had. But beyond that, the rule refers back to a more general rule, to a way of life. To speak and write well, you must live well—which means in tune with the world rather than in isolation, perceptive rather than shut up in your own self. How can you have stories and small talk and vivid descriptions on tap if you never paid much attention to what went on? How can you quote people's exact words if you never properly listen to what they say? How can you make other people see what you haven't really seen yourself?

Communication works like everything else: output depends on intake. Effective speaking and writing depends on effective listening and reading—and even more on effective seeing, hearing, feeling, and doing. If you feel that your command of English isn't up to par, the real reason is probably that you go through life half asleep. Wake up! Go out and get material to talk and write about. Find out who, what, when, where, and why. The world is made of specific details.

6

Poetry and Punctuation

The pause—*that impressive silence, that eloquent silence, that geometrically progressive silence which often achieves a desired effect where no combination of words howsoever felicitous could accomplish it.*

—MARK TWAIN

MOLIÈRE'S MONSIEUR JOURDAIN WAS surprised when he was told he had been speaking prose all his life without knowing it. He would have been even more surprised had someone told him that throughout his life he had been unconsciously a poet. And yet, the second statement is just as true as the first.

All of us at times, when carried away by emotion, break into poetry. We are fighting mad, or madly in love, or desperately worried, and our words shape themselves into patterns, arrange themselves rhythmically, flow with unpremeditated power. "Stop it! Stop it! Stop it!" we cry in anguish—and it's a poem. "A year ago I didn't know your name" we say softly— and it's blank verse. "I haven't had a minute's rest for months" we complain—and it's still blank verse.

What's the difference between poetry and prose? Look it
up in all the scholarly books, and you'll find that nobody
knows. Poetry is love, prose is justice, says one writer; poetry
is static, prose is progressive, says another. "Poetry is creative
expression; prose is constructive expression," says Herbert
Read; and Logan Pearsall Smith writes: "If I were tempted to
draw a distinction . . . I should not be disinclined to say that
while poetry is primarily addressed to imaginative feeling, prose
is best fitted to appeal to imaginative reason."

All of which means simply that it's impossible to draw a
line—or that nobody so far has managed to do it to everybody
else's satisfaction. We make a shadowy distinction between
poetry and prose—and what it comes down to is that there
are certain qualities that make human utterances more or less
poetic or prosaic.

Is the Bible prose or poetry? You'll answer that some parts
are one, some the other. Well, what about the Book of
Daniel? Prose, you say—and technically speaking, you are
right. But listen to Daniel's prayer, for instance:

> O Lord, according to all thy righteousness, I beseech thee,
> let thine anger and thy fury be turned away from the city
> Jerusalem, thy holy mountain: because for our sins, and for
> the iniquities of our fathers, Jerusalem and thy people are
> become a reproach to all that are about us.
>
> Now therefore, O our God, hear the prayer of thy servant,
> and his supplications, and cause thy face to shine upon thy
> sanctuary that is desolate, for the Lord's sake.
>
> O my God, incline thine ear, and hear; open thine eyes,
> and behold our desolations, and the city which is called by
> thy name: for we do not present our supplications before
> thee for our righteousnesses, but for thy great mercies.

O Lord, hear; O Lord, forgive; O Lord, hearken and do;
defer not, for thine own sake, O my God: for thy city and
thy people are called by thy name.

Prose? Hardly. I say it's poetry, even if it doesn't fit any
definition anyone ever thought up.

Or—to go from the Bible to the nineteenth century—what
about Walt Whitman? Yes, you admit that Whitman's verse
was irregular—but still, you say, it was clearly poetry and not
prose. All right, let's have a look at Walt Whitman's *prose*—
say, his *Democratic Vistas*:

We see our land, America, her literature, esthetics, etc.,
as, substantially, the getting in form, or effusement and
statement, of deepest basic elements and loftiest final mean-
ings, of history and man—and the portrayal (under the
eternal laws and conditions of beauty) of our own physiog-
nomy, the subjective tie and expression of the objective, as
from our own combination, continuation, and points of
view—and the deposit and record of the national mentality,
character, appeals, heroism, wars, and even liberties—where
these, and all, culminate in native literary and artistic formulation, to be perpetuated; and not having which native,
first-class formulation, she will flounder about, and her
other, however imposing, eminent greatness, prove merely
a passing gleam; but truly having which, she will understand
herself, live nobly, nobly contribute, emanate, and, swing-
ing, poised safely on herself, illumined and illumining, become a full-formed world, and divine Mother not only of
material but spiritual worlds, in ceaseless succession through
time—the main thing being the average, the bodily, the concrete, the democratic, the popular, on which all the super-
structures of the future are to permanently rest.

After digressing for a moment to point out that this last paragraph from one of America's greatest literary landmarks ends in a triumphant, ringing, echoing split infinitive—and after earnestly recommending that this paragraph, framed and printed in large clear type, should be put on the desks of all the country's English teachers for them to daily, weekly and permanently look at—I shall assert that it is poetry. Prose, to be sure, but poetry too, since it was written by Walt Whitman who was constitutionally unable to be prosaic.

Finally, to take a contemporary example, here is America's great twentieth-century poet, Thomas Wolfe. It so happened that this poet wrote prose—but what kind of prose!

Oh, softly, softly, the great dark horses of Sleep are galloping over the land. The tides of Sleep are moving in the hearts of men, they flow like rivers in the night, they flow with glut and fullness of their dark, unfathomed strength into a million pockets of the land and over the shores of the whole earth. They flow with the full might of their advancing and inexorable flood across the continent of night, across the breadth and sweep of the immortal earth, until the hearts of all men living are relieved of their harsh weight, the souls of all men who have ever drawn in the breath of anguish and of labor are healed, assuaged, and conquered by the vast enchantments of dark, silent, all-engulfing Sleep.

Sleep falls like silence on the earth, it fills the hearts of ninety million men, it moves like magic in the mountains, and walks like night and darkness across the plains and rivers of the earth, until low upon lowlands, and high upon hills, flows gently sleep, smooth-sliding sleep—oh, sleep—sleep—sleep!

Poetry is a matter of degree. The author of the Book of Daniel, and Walt Whitman, and Thomas Wolfe were poets; what they said and wrote was poetry. Most of us, in most of our moments, are prosaic people, and what comes out of our mouths and typewriters is prose. But poetry exists within us: we never know when our words will start to dance—break into sudden rhythms here and there—arrange themselves in little plays and games—or march with heavy, solemn, massive tread.

When we write like that, and want to show the reader what we are about, we call upon the help of punctuation. Spoken poetry is always understood as poetry; but in writing the reader must be told to watch out for the rhythm, or he may miss it. So, by tradition, we label poetry by printing it in a special way, starting new lines at certain conventional points; and we call poetry whatever is printed in that fashion. But as I have shown, there is poetry all around us, mixed up with almost every piece of written prose, and for that poetic aspect of prose we need punctuation. The three examples I quoted cry out to be printed like poetry—that is, as a succession of separate, rhythmically divided verses; but even more than that, they cannot be properly read without punctuation. They wouldn't mean the same thing to us if their poetic quality were not brought out by commas, colons, and dashes.

That's why punctuation is so important. There is poetry in almost all prose, and poetry is essentially spoken. It needs rhythm, intonation, stress, and pitch to be fully understood.

Poetry on paper is merely a makeshift; it would not even be that if we had no punctuation.

But that is absurd, you say. Punctuation isn't as glorious as all that. It's the words that count; and in poetry it's the images, the metaphors, the pictures and colors and sounds. Punctuation is a trifle; it's ridiculous to blow it up into something out of all proportion.

To which I answer that your point of view is all wrong. You look at punctuation as a nasty little appendix to grammar, pesky rules you learned in school about commas and quotation marks—the kind of thing a good secretary is supposed to know about and, if necessary, add to her boss's letters and memos. In your mind, punctuation and spelling go hand in hand—people with thick glasses sit in ivory towers and count the commas in Chaucer while those outside go about the world's business.

You are wrong. To prove to you that you are wrong, I have to go back into history—way, way back, right to the beginning:

There, in the dawn of history, we see the first human beings communicating with each other. They use their early primitive words; they make themselves understood by gesticulating, by raising their voices, by singing and chanting, by yelling and whispering, by long silences punctuated by sudden floods of rapid, urgently uttered speech; they walk up and down, they jump in the air, they embrace each other or act out what they are saying; they intersperse their words with all sorts of un-classifiable, meaningful, spur-of-the-moment sounds. They *communicate*; they bridge the gap between two human beings by a hundred and one different means, one of which is the succession of words and sentences. For their needs, the system is wonderfully effective: what they want to communicate is their emotions, the way they feel. They discover that language works; which means to them that face-to-face talk works— words accompanied by whatever other emotional expression is handy.

Now, having remembered the basic truth that language is essentially speech, that communication is essentially face-to-face talk, think of oral communication today. Think of actors, of political speakers, of preachers, of door-to-door salesmen: what is the secret of their language effectiveness? Their vocabulary? Their syntax? Their logic? Don't be ridiculous. Ask one of them and he'll immediately tell you. The secret of effective speech lies in delivery. A crack salesman, as you know, can sell you a dozen left ski boots and a ten-year subscription to the *Grandchildren's Digest*; a great actor can make you cry like a baby by reading aloud from the telephone book. In this respect, things today are just as they were thirty thousand years ago: in face-to-face talk what counts is not the words but the delivery.

Which brings us back to punctuation. For what is punctuation? It's a system of symbols to show how written and printed language should be delivered orally. Commas, periods, dashes are clues—for those who are going to read aloud as well as for those who are going to read silently to themselves. These clues tell us in what rhythm we should read, where we should insert pauses, and at what points we should raise or lower our voice. If we want to bring out the emotional force of the pattern and arrangement of the words, we must follow the clues of the punctuation. Without punctuation, we would have just the words; with punctuation, we have some of the power and effectiveness those words would have if the writer spoke to us in person.

Unfortunately, however, our system of punctuation gives us just a tiny fraction of the means by which everybody increases the emotional power of words. We use commas for certain brief pauses in our speech; we use periods at the end of sentences; we use colons and semicolons for certain special purposes. We start a new paragraph on a new line. We use, sparingly, dashes, parentheses, and series of dots; we sometimes underline or italicize words. And that's all. That's practically our whole repertory for putting on paper clues on how to deliver written language. It's pitiful; it makes it all but impossible to convey any of the thousand ways in which a given set of words can be read; but that's what we have and nobody seems to think that anything could or should be done about it.

Why not branch out? Why not, for example, print or write poetic prose like poetry, in rhythmic "takes"? This has been done for some of Thomas Wolfe's prose; it has been used for Winston Churchill's speeches to give him clues for their delivery. Why not make this a more common practice? Why not use inverted question marks and exclamation points at the beginning as well as at the end of questions and exclamations, the way it's done in Spanish? Why not occasionally use s p a c i n g for added emphasis, the way it is used in German? Why not make consistent use of other symbols—say, the paragraph sign (¶) for itemized listing or the ∴ symbol for logical conclusions? Why not—to make a frankly revolutionary suggestion—take the system of punctuation we have now and use it the way it was meant to be used?

For the fact is, we are not even properly using the few punctuation symbols we do have. They *can* be used to bring out the poetry in prose, to show rhythm and pattern and emotional movement; they have been used that way for centuries. But not any more. Somewhere in the course of history we took a wrong turn and shifted from rhythmical to grammatical punctuation. We don't punctuate our sentences today the way Shakespeare punctuated his or the authors of the King James Version of the Bible punctuated theirs. We call their system old-fashioned: actually, they knew how to use punctuation marks and we don't.

I tried to find out who was responsible for the shift from free rhythmical punctuation to the rigid grammatical system we have today—who deserves the laurels in this field that correspond to those of Bishop Lowth in the field of grammar. I am not sure; but I am herewith pointing an accusing finger at Mr. John Wilson, a printer who published a *Treatise on English Punctuation* in 1844. The Wilson treatise immediately became the bible of punctuation; it ran into over thirty editions and has been, directly or indirectly, the source of practically everything that has been written about punctuation since.

The comma-happy spirit of Wilson's work can be shown best by a brief quotation:

> In nouns, we think, the comma is usually required, to show that the terms, which might otherwise be regarded as significant of two ideas or things, are designed to represent only one and the same; but the pointing of adjectives and adverbs similarly situated would, in many cases, tend, by the breaking-up of the connection, to confuse, instead of assisting, the reader.

(Which corresponds closely to a sentence Lord Dunsany once constructed to show what printers would do to writers if they had it all their own way: "Moreover, Jones, who, as, indeed, you, probably, know, is, of course, Welsh, is, perhaps, coming, too, but, unfortunately, alone.")

Before the Wilson-type grammatical punctuation was invented, we had something entirely different. It was simple; it was beautiful; and it gave writers full freedom to use punctuation as they saw fit.

There is no better description of the classic system of punctuation than the one by its inventor (or at least, its first consistent user), the Venetian printer Aldus Manutius. Here is what Aldus Manutius wrote in 1566:

> Let us proceed, as it were by steps, from the lowest of the points to the highest.
>
> The least degree of separation is indicated by the comma.
>
> This same mark, if it is used along with a single point, as this is (;) is found in passages in which the words are not opposed in meaning, but the sense depends on the words in such a way, that, if you use the comma it is too little; if the double points, too much. I was thinking to give an example: but, I felt the point had come out plainly enough, in the immediately preceding sentence.
>
> The doubling of the point is next to be considered: the effect of this doubling is, that the mark thus formed takes rank between the point used in conjunction with the comma, and the point standing alone.
>
> There remains the single point, with which the sentence is closed, and completed. It is not difficult to understand for one cannot fail to notice with what word a sentence ends although, when it is short and another short one follows, I myself use the double point more freely than the single, as for instance: *Make ready a lodging for me: for I shall*

arrive tomorrow: and so again: *I give you no orders concerning my affairs: you yourself will decide what is to be done.*

In other words, the old system of punctuation was built upon a simple series of pauses: a comma stood for one unit, a semicolon for two, a colon for three, and a period for four. That was all. It was up to each writer to use the system to show whatever rhythm he happened to use.

Present-day Americans know this system, if at all, only as the Bible system of punctuation, having vaguely wondered from time to time why there are so many colons and semicolons in the Bible. The explanation is simple: the authors of the King James Version used the old system, and they used it to perfection. I quoted a few sentences from the Book of Daniel earlier in this chapter. Look at them again—or look at this from the Fifth Chapter of the Gospel of St. John:

> Verily, verily, I say unto you, The hour is coming, and now is, when the dead shall hear the voice of the son of God: and they that hear shall live.
>
> For as the Father hath life in himself; so hath he given to the Son to have life in himself;
>
> And hath given him authority to execute judgment also, because he is the Son of man.
>
> Marvel not at this: for the hour is coming, in the which all that are in the graves shall hear his voice,
>
> And shall come forth; they that have done good, unto the resurrection of life; and they that have done evil, unto the resurrection of damnation.
>
> I can of mine own self do nothing: as I hear, I judge: and my judgment is just; because I seek not mine own will, but the will of the Father which hath sent me.

Not one of these colons and semicolons is arbitrary; and not one is used for the sake of any grammatical distinction. They mean exactly what they are supposed to mean according to Aldus Manutius' system: a colon stands for a pause not quite as long as that following a period; a semicolon means a pause that is one split second shorter. Read the passage aloud, following the four-unit system to the letter. You will see.

And now you may ask: "If this was the system used around 1600, why wasn't it used in Shakespeare's plays?" Shakespeare, you remember dimly, does *not* have all those Bible colons and semicolons; why not?

The answer is to be found in Mr. Percy Simpson's fascinating book on *Shakespearean Punctuation*. What happened was this: Shakespeare did use the classic, or Bible, system and the plays were printed according to that system in the famous First Folio of 1623. But in the succeeding centuries the printers somehow took charge of punctuation, and by and by they repunctuated Shakespeare. Look at your own edition and you'll find it's all properly punctuated according to the latest textbooks.

Mr. Simpson, naturally, considered such a practice sheer sacrilege. He firmly believed that Shakespeare himself wrote every single comma that was printed in the First Folio—and that those commas were just as much a work of genius as his words. He quoted evidence: dozens, scores, hundreds of lines that show the hand of the master in using punctuation.

For example, Brutus says in *Julius Caesar*: "As Caesar loved me, I weep for him; as he was fortunate, I rejoice at it; as he was valiant, I honour him: but, as he was ambitious, I slew him." (My modern edition has a semicolon instead of the colon after "I honour him," robbing Shakespeare of his climactic longer pause.)

Or these lines from *King Richard II*:

> As gentle, and as jocund, as to jest,
> Go I to fight: truth, has a quiet breast.

(The only comma I find in my modern edition is the one after *jest*; the others—Shakespeare's exact indications of short rhythmical pauses—are today considered "ungrammatical." The comma after *truth*—between a subject and its predicate—would fill every schoolteacher in the land with speechless horror.)

This is from *Romeo and Juliet*:

> Or if thou think'st I am too quickly won,
> I'll frown and be perverse, and say thee nay,
> So thou wilt woo: but else not for the world.

(Shakespeare has here a long-pause colon after *woo*, and no comma after *else*, which makes a charming and meaningful contrast in rhythm; my modern edition has a semicolon after *woo* and a comma after *else*—which makes Juliet sound more logical but less kittenish.)

Again from *Romeo and Juliet*:

"Love, is the smoke made with the fume of sighs." (Another of those commas between subject and predicate that are today considered unforgivable sins.)

And the lines on which *Romeo and Juliet* ends:

> For never was a story of more woe,
> Than this of Juliet, and her Romeo.

(Compare Shakespeare's original rhythm with this curtain line from my modern edition:

> For never was a story of more woe
> Than this of Juliet and her Romeo.

Without the commas it's a jingle.)

You see? Shakespeare enjoyed the seventeenth-century freedom of punctuation and used it to the hilt; if he lived today, he would have to fight the whole typographers' union to get a single one of those commas onto paper.

In the eighteenth century the classic system of punctuation apparently declined. Still, there were free spirits like Laurence Sterne, who followed their own bent. (Consequently, Sterne is put in his place in a scholarly footnote to the introduction of my 1940 edition of *Tristram Shandy*: "The punctuation is oral rather than syntactical; Sterne was a talker, not a grammarian.")

This is a typical paragraph from *Tristram Shandy*:

> Digressions, incontestably, are the sunshine;—they are the life, the soul of reading;—take them out of this book for instance,—you might as well take the book along with them;—one cold eternal winter would reign in every page of it; restore them to the writer;—he steps forth like a bridegroom,—bids All hail; brings in variety, and forbids the appetite to fail.

But where are the days when such a thing was still possible? Here we are today, and everybody has to use the same kind of punctuation or else. No freedom, no individual rhythm, nothing but grammatical rules, you must do this and you mustn't do that. Those beautiful semicolons and colons have practically disappeared, and what we get in most books, magazines, and newspapers is a steady succession of neatly complete, primly grammatical sentences, each ending chastely in the universal, standardized period. To a seventeenth-century reader, this would imply that we all nowadays speak with pauses of exactly the same length; and maybe it's true that our speech has gotten more monotonous and more prosaic in its rhythm.

In the course of the past six or eight years I have accumulated quite a collection of English textbooks. They range from good to bad to infuriating. To illustrate my point, I shall now quote from a college text in the "infuriating" classification.

The very first thing the unhappy college freshman finds in that text is a long discussion of the "sentence fragment." And *what* a discussion! There is a list of twenty-four perfectly nice, pleasant constructions that are exposed as vicious and sinful and shown how to behave themselves properly. For instance: "Everyone arrived late. Too late. The speaker had given up and gone home." (*Error!*, cries my textbook. Make it: "Everyone arrived late. In fact, everyone arrived too late. The speaker had given up and gone home.") Or this: "All work and no play. Eventually you will have to take a rest—in a sanitarium!" (An essential part has been omitted, it says here. *Correct*: "All work and no play wears down the nervous system. Eventually you will have to take a rest—in a sanitarium!") Or this: "There were times when I absolutely refused to walk down that lonely road. During darkness, for instance." (No good, says my text. Correct the error: "There were times when I absolutely refused to walk down that lonely road. A dark night was one of those times.")

Why English teachers are so horrified by sentence frag-

ments, I don't know. Must be another one of those neuroses
I mentioned, I suppose. And it would be so easy to cure them!
Just make them understand once and for all that here is a
twentieth-century remnant of the old system of rhythmical
punctuation. What those poor innocent students tried to do
was simply to indicate a long pause in the middle of a sentence—or in some other place where there didn't happen to be
a *grammatical* reason for putting down a period. What's wrong
with that? Their "sentence fragments" were exact records of
their thought and emotional meaning. The "corrected" sentences are not.

Just yesterday I read an excellent example of one of those
"faulty sentence fragments." Here it is: "They were, of course,
seen by everybody. But especially by a certain old lady named
Mrs. Quigley, who made the purveying of gossip her business."
Luckily, the perpetrator of this ghastly sin is beyond the reach
of English teachers' red pencils. It's from a short story by
Bertrand Russell, eighty-year-old Nobel prize winner in
literature.

But let's move on to something else. Says my infuriating
textbook: "The *comma fault* is the name given to the error
of separating two independent clauses by only a comma."
Whereupon it quotes examples of this horrible vice: "It was
a cold, dreary day, leaves hung limply from the trees."—"I
have never seen the word before, so I don't know what it
means."—"The trains run on time, the old-fashioned buses are
frequently late." The guilty students are given an option of
either replacing the commas by periods or by semicolons or by
commas plus *and*. But would that serve their obvious purpose? Would that indicate that the paired sentences, in their
own minds, were only a heartbeat apart, with just barely room

enough for a comma? Of course not. The student sentences
are examples of good rhythmical punctuation; the professor's
replacements are stuffy grammatical statements.

If my textbook author is interested in some really good examples of "comma faults," I would recommend an attentive
reading of *Cry, the Beloved Country* by Alan Paton, widely
known as one of the great literary masterpieces of this century.

He paused for a moment, then he said, I do not wish to
offend you gentlemen, but the Church too is like the chief.
You must do so and so and so. You are not free to have an
experience. A man must be faithful and meek and obedient,
and he must obey the laws, whatever the laws may be. It is
true that the Church speaks with a fine voice, and that the
Bishops speak against the laws. But this they have been
doing for fifty years, and things get worse, not better.

Call oh small boy, with the long tremulous cry that
echoes over the hills. Dance oh small boy, with the first
slow steps of the dance that is for yourself. Call and dance,
Innocence, call and dance while you may. For this is a
prelude, it is only a beginning. Strange things will be woven
into it, by men you have never heard of, in places you have
never seen. It is life you are going into, you are not afraid
because you do not know. Call and dance, call and dance.
Now, while you may.

And what about the rhythmical use of the colon and semicolon? These matters aren't even mentioned in a modern
textbook any more. In my pet book the model use of the colon
and the semicolon is shown like this: "Americans prefer to
spell the word thus: *color*; the British, *colour*." And: "This
poem is bad; that, good."

Compare this emasculated prose with that of Bernard Shaw, the only great modern user of the rhythmical colon and semicolon. This is from *Saint Joan*:

> I believe that God is wiser than I; and it is His commands that I will do. All the things that you call my crimes have come to me by the command of God. I say that I have done them by the order of God: it is impossible for me to say anything else. If any Churchman says the contrary I shall not mind him: I shall mind God alone, whose command I always follow.

Is it too late to regain our freedom of punctuation? I don't think so. It may not be possible to reconquer the pure system of Aldus Manutius; but it is surely possible to throw overboard all those preposterous rules set up God knows when by over-fussy printers. Why can't I use a colon after this sentence: who says I can't? Why can't we have sentence fragments galore, and comma faults, and wild and woolly punctuation à la Laurence Sterne, and fun and rhythm and a little poetry? Why can't we get some air onto our written and printed pages? It's stuffy in here: there are all those commas and periods, shutting off the air.

So look at your prose and think about its delivery. How do you talk? With proper emphasis? With many expressive pauses? With fortes and pianissimos, with staccatos and legatos, with a variety of pitch and stress and rhythm? Does your voice, your face, your body say what your words say? Do you smile, do you frown, do you shrug your shoulders, do you stamp your feet and wave your arms?

Probably not—or not all the time, at least. But some of these things you do, and you could do more of them if you were willing to overcome your inhibitions. Make them listen to you; make them watch your antics. You want to make your point, don't you? All right, work at it. Reading a string of sentences from a sheet of paper is the lazy man's way to talk. It won't set the world on fire—it won't even make a single customer spend a nickel for peanuts.

And now think about your writing. Punctuation is what in writing stands for delivery, remember. Look over the punctuation marks available to you today and see what you can do with them. Never mind those arbitrary printers' rules and those ridiculous textbooks with their sentence fragments and comma faults and whatnot. You are a free citizen of the United States, aren't you? Nobody can tell you how to deliver your words, whether spoken or written. Use punctuation to make your readers sit up and notice. What good are your words and your splendid ideas if they all sound like a dripping faucet?

Let's start with the comma—yes, the humble, insignificant comma. Remember Lord Dunsany's horrible example I quoted on page 113; "Moreover, Jones, who, as, indeed, you, probably, know, is, of course, Welsh, is, perhaps, coming, too, but, unfortunately, alone." You don't have to write like that—in spite of what the rulebooks say. You can write that whole sentence without a single comma, if that's the way you would *say* it. Put commas where you make brief pauses; leave them out where there are *no* pauses between your words. If you need reassurance, let me tell you that according to the researches of Dr. George Summey, Jr., author of the excellent book *American Punctuation* (Ronald Press, 1949), the use of commas has dropped sharply in the last fifty years. Now more and more publications are printed the way people talk.

If you are the kind of person who writes "But, the situation has changed," forget about the comma after *but*: it's out of date. (Unless, of course, you want to indicate a pause.) If you hesitate to write "Well I don't know" without the traditional comma after *well*, take the plunge. Use the comma only if you would *say* it—that is, if you would pause after *well*; if not, leave it out.

Let's go on—to the period, the semicolon, the colon. Don't let them tell you the semicolon is an old-fashioned mark, now out of date. It isn't so. The news-weeklies, and all other publications that use short emphatic sentences, have rediscovered it years ago. Look through *Time* and watch how they use periods for longer pauses and semicolons for shorter pauses between sentences, following old Aldus Manutius to the letter. "By the middle of last month the wide-screen revolution was looking more and more like an inventory sale; the three-dimensional revolution had still not proven itself to be anything more than a freak show; and Hollywood was in confusion, with production at a standstill." You see what the semicolons do? They make it dramatic. Without them it would be a mumbling tale: with them, it's alive. The same with colons: look at this sentence and the preceding one. See what I mean? Reach for the semicolons and colons and learn how to use them. Be dramatic. Make it exciting. Don't put exactly the same pauses between all your sentences.

Next, the paragraph. The paragraph is what comes next in the series of pauses—comma, semicolon, colon, period, paragraph. Use it that way. Again, never mind the textbooks. They will tell you that paragraphing is a mystical art, involving the recognition of mysterious units of ideas that must be separated by starting on a new line. Nonsense. Paragraphs *can* be used that way, but they don't have to. Just like periods, you can use paragraphs for effect in the *middle* of a thought unit. You can write "I like people. Especially women" and the period will be several dozen times more effective than a comma. Do the same with paragraphs.

Right in the middle of your thought, when you get to the climax, start on a new line. The way I did right now. It's effective, it's unconventional, it's dramatic. Why not do it from time to time? Why not stop for a climactic pause just when your reader least expects it? Ask any old-fashioned spell-binding orator whether that isn't a good way to make them listen.

The classic system of punctuation had four marks for pauses. You are much better off. Not only do you have the paragraph, for extra length, but you also have the dash—a wonderful all-purpose instrument, which you can use as the spirit moves you. If you don't like it, you don't have to use it at all, confining yourself to the regular series from the comma to the paragraph. But if you want to—a world of opportunities is open to you. Use dashes for parenthetical thoughts—like this, for instance—or use them for whimsical digressions—why am I getting so hungry as I am writing this? —or use them for rhythmical, musical effects—to end a sentence softly—softly—softly—

Why don't people use more dashes? I know: it's "undignified," it "isn't done," it looks sentimental and effusive. Which means, actually, nothing but that people nowadays are afraid to show their feelings, to come out of their reserve, to speak and write as if they meant what they said. How do you expect to make sense to anybody, to win friends and influence people with your ideas, if you don't get behind those ideas with your own voice, your manner, the *way* you speak and write? If, in your imagination, you would pause and pound on the desk—well, then at least mark that pause with a dash in writing.

And what about question marks? What about exclamation points? The same thing all over again. They seem to be dying out in our culture. "There appears to be a question as to the recent drop in sales" we write in a low murmur, not raising our voice an inch. What we would *like* to say is this: "What in God's name has happened? Why did we take such a beating last year?" We want to know; questions tumble from our lips; but nary a question mark interrupts the pristine series of periods on our pages.

And exclamation points? We have put them on a special shelf, to be used solely by schoolgirls, novelists, and copywriters. "They are milder! It contains multifume!!" What's the matter with the rest of us? Can't we get excited about *anything* any more? Is enthusiasm now reserved for movies, beer, and cigarettes? I don't believe it. In fact, I am writing this on a typewriter that was sold with an exclamation point on its regular keyboard—"for students, writers, teachers." Glory be! The day will come when exclamation points will become the property of everybody once more—of housewives, businessmen, and even government officials.

Punctuation means even more. It also means italics for emphasis. Why not underline the words you would stress in speaking? The answer is again the same. You're afraid it would spoil the dignity of your letter, your report, your edict from on high to the waiting world. Forget it. Remember President Theodore Roosevelt, who had a clever trick of underlining key words in his letters with *ink*, giving the addressee a wonderful warm feeling that the President of the United States personally went out of his way to show him the significance of those words. Don't tell me that you are a better human relations expert than Theodore Roosevelt was: I won't believe it.

You can even show an undertone and a light touch by punctuation: you can use parentheses for casual asides. Do you think parentheses look heavy? They don't. They can be as light as paper clips (or as butterfly wings, if you want to be poetic). They are there, for you to use. Indicate your delivery on paper. Don't just sit there and mumble in a monotone all the time.

Don't hand your words to your reader in an undramatic, uninteresting, pauseless sequence, like this gem I found in a newspaper:

> Although the music dramas of Wagner remain among the mainstays of the Metropolitan Opera Association's repertoire and concerts of excerpts from them are rarer nowadays than was the case not so many years ago there is still much pleasure to be derived from such a concert when it is devised as intelligently as the one planned for the Philadelphia Orchestra in Carnegie Hall last night by Eugene Ormandy, but conducted by his associate, Alexander Hilsberg, because Mr. Ormandy was suffering from a virus infection.

Rather, learn from the newest literary invention, the newsletter. Write like this for a change:

> What about high wage costs—can selling prices come down while these are up?
> New machinery, new automatic industrial control systems require fewer men than older methods.

Example: New 250,000 kilowatt electric energy plant on eastern seaboard has total manpower of 85—including eight operators per shift.

Same system has another plant same size—but five years old. It requires 120 men.

Does this mean machinery replaces men? No. More plants, more men, more output at less wage cost per unit.

In other words, recognize the great truth that in all communication delivery means as much as content, and more. Put forth your argument as if it were the result of six months of research and of consultations with Albert Einstein and the whole nine-man Supreme Court—convey *by your manner* the utmost of faith and conviction—and people will hang on your lips. Do the same in writing. Don't let yourself be hogtied by vague, unwritten laws decreeing that all sentences must end in a period, or that dashes, italics, and exclamation points cannot be worn in the presence of elderly, respectable readers.

Go ahead. Write without commas if you feel like it and want to talk about a breathless sequence of men women children houses bridges cars buses trucks trees rocks rivers mountains and trains rumbling faraway at night. Write in run-on sentences, they have their uses, they show the steady movement of ideas, they push forward, they follow one another with mounting emphasis, they form a train of thought, they carry forward what you mean, they approach their destination, they arrive. Write in sentence fragments. For drama. For excitement. For interruptions. For a change of pace. For hammer blows. For trumpets. For conviction.

Use semicolons for your short emphatic pauses; use them to add new rhythm to your writing; find out what they can do. Use colons: they are stagy, dramatic, they have an air of high expectancy. Use many paragraphs—leave white space for the reader's thoughts.

Remember that short paragraphs have more effect than long ones. Don't hesitate to make a paragraph out of only three sentences or two.

Or even one.

Don't try to speak and write like everybody else. Be yourself. Be a poet if you feel like being poetic, be a preacher if you feel like preaching a sermon. Never mind the punctuation rules of the English teachers and the printers.

Listen to *yourself*.

Put it down the way you'd *say* it.

7

On Feedback, Semantic Noise, and Redundancy

There are some who speak well and write badly. For the place and the audience warms them, and draws from their minds more than they think of without that warmth.

—Pascal, Pensées

THIS CHAPTER AT FIRST HAD A DIFFERENT TITLE. But my wife asked me what it was going to be about and I told her about feedback, semantic noise, and redundancy. Whereupon she insisted I should use those words in the title. So I did.

"Feedback," "semantic noise," and "redundancy" are intriguing words. They were thought up by mathematicians. Applied to such unmathematical pursuits as speaking and writing, they give you the feeling they will open up brand-new vistas and provide totally unexpected insights. And that's exactly what they do.

I came upon the feedback principle first in the revolutionary book *Cybernetics* by Dr. Norbert Wiener that stirred up so much comment a few years ago. Cybernetics is a word coined by Dr. Wiener for the science of the automatic control of behavior; the book carries the fascinating subtitle "Control and Communication in the Animal and the Machine."

Dr. Wiener has the exciting trick of always talking about the behavior of human beings and machines in the same breath; everything he says is full of startling parallels and surprising applications. The feedback principle, he explains, underlies practically everything human beings do as well as everything automatic machines do. He defines it like this: "The feedback principle means that behavior is scanned for its result, and that the success or failure of this result modifies future behavior."

What does this mean? Let's take two examples, one from the realm of human beings and one from that of automatic machines. Imagine yourself picking up a pencil from a desk. Your eyes locate the position of the pencil, your brain issues the necessary commands to your nervous system, and you stretch out your hand. As your hand approaches the pencil, your eyes register that fact and report back to the brain. Information is *fed back*. On the basis of that feedback, your brain issues new, revised commands to your nervous system and the muscles of your arm and hand until finally, when your eyes report that your hand is exactly above the pencil, your fingers are directed to reach down and grasp it. The feedback therefore makes it possible for you to behave in such a way as to accomplish your purpose. Every human being has a million built-in feedback automatisms—they are the basic mechanism of human life.

Now let's look at a piece of machinery with a built-in feedback. Probably the most widely known and used automatic mechanism is a thermostat. How does the feedback work here? Like this: The furnace in the basement heats the house. The thermostat in the living room registers the temperature. When the room temperature reaches 70—if that's what you have set it for—the thermostat feeds that information back to the furnace and tells it to stop furnishing heat. In this way the machine uses the feedback to accomplish *its* purpose.

The feedback principle applies to all automatic machinery of any kind—it's what makes a mechanism automatic. It also, as I said, applies to all animals and human beings—automatic response to our environment comes natural to us; it's the way we are made. So, since the feedback principle has to do with communication and the exchange of information, it applies specifically to everything that has to do with communication between human beings: that is, to speaking, reading, and writing.

Once you start thinking about speaking and writing in terms of the feedback, a great many things become startlingly clear. You realize that the effectiveness of speech and writing depends largely—maybe entirely—on whether the feedback is in good working order. Without the feedback your words may never hit the target—like your hand not reaching or over-shooting that pencil. Your writing may not be read or understood because its direction may have been wrong—and there was no feedback information to let you know about it. In short, the feedback is the automatic control that is absolutely necessary to make sure your words have conveyed meaning to someone else's mind.

Let's take a simple case: You make a speech in a large hall filled with people. You start talking, and it turns out that your voice doesn't carry to the back of the hall. Whereupon someone back there shouts "Louder!", other people join in, and within ten seconds two dozen voices cry "Louder! Louder! Louder!" You raise your voice, the cries of "Louder!" stop, and you go on from there, exerting yourself to make a bigger noise.

That's a laboratory specimen of the feedback. You started talking in a certain way, using your vocal chords in a certain manner. Your audience fed you back the information that that didn't work: communication didn't get through. So you acted on the basis of that feedback, changed certain aspects of your speaking behavior, and the error was corrected. From there on you could accomplish your purpose and convey your meaning to everybody present.

Now let's apply the same principle to the *contents* of speech rather than the mechanics of its transmission. Logically, if the feedback applies to communication in general, it applies also to grammar, vocabulary, style, form of presentation, subject matter—in short, to everything. To be one-hundred per cent effective, you should rely on the feedback to determine your words, your sentences, your illustrations, whether to stop or go on, and whether to use a happy or unhappy ending.

Let's say you are telling a story to a child. You mention a dog and you make him say "Wooff! Wooff!" The child's face lights up, clearly indicating that "Wooff! Wooff!" has made a hit. So you get lavish in conversational openings for the dog in your story; then you branch out and add a cat that says repeatedly "Mee-aoow! Mee-aoow!"; then you add a cow, a donkey, a rooster, and a choo-choo train; and by the time you are through, the feedback principle has produced an entirely unplanned, wildly successful performance.

That's exactly the sort of thing that must have happened

when language was in its early stages. The head of the family, coming back from a tribal war—I seem to be using nothing but caveman examples in this book, but how else can you talk about the fundamentals of communication than by starting at the natural beginning?—the returning stone-age warrior tells of his exploits to the assembled circle of gaping womenfolk and children. Two minutes after he has started, the feedback begins to operate: Appreciative noises from the audience show that there ought to be some more highlights of the hand-to-hand fighting, exclamations indicate that further gruesome details will be welcomed, an ominous silence at other points suggests a sharp condensation of less interesting descriptive material. So the tale shapes itself following the demands of the audience. When it is told a second time—and a third—and a tenth—the repeated feedback has done its work: maybe there is considerably less truth in it now, but it sure makes a wonderful story.

From which example you can see that there is a subtle and highly dangerous relationship between feedback and truth. But before we get into that question, let's consider the following basic fact: The feedback principle, as you see, operates only in direct oral communication, in face-to-face talk. It does not work where there is no audience present—which means particularly that it does not work in writing. And since, as I said, the effectiveness of communication depends largely on the feedback, this means that *the basic problem in writing is that there is no feedback.*

Consider this carefully. It has enormous implications. It makes you realize that writing at bottom is something like squaring the circle; it's something that cannot be done but is done every day; it's the performance of the impossible.

For there is no getting away from the fact that the basic language activity is face-to-face talk. Everything else is derived from it. In face-to-face talk you not only raise and lower your voice according to the reaction of your audience, you also choose your words and your grammatical constructions that way, you insert pauses or speed up your narrative, you add details and illustrations, you shape the whole content of what you say. In writing there is no audience in front of you; there is only the imagined reader or readers who will see what you are now writing after days or weeks or months have passed. The invention of writing has made it possible for you to reach that invisible audience, but in doing so it has deprived you of the feedback. You are on your own. There is nothing and nobody to tell you how to say it, what to say, how to start, how to go on, how to finish. There is no applause or laughter you can hear and no yawning you can see. Nature has provided you with the beautiful instrument of the feedback to make you talk as effectively as possible; but civilization has taken that instrument away from you. There you sit, robbed of the most essential thing you need to reach an audience.

There is only one way to solve this basic dilemma involved in all writing—or at least to approach some sort of solution: you must supply the missing feedback out of your memory or imagination. You must see that invisible audience before you as you write; you must imagine, with the utmost powers of your imagination, how that audience will behave, what they are going to like, what they are going to dislike, whether they will interrupt you with questions, whether they will ask for more of this or less of that, whether they will need an interval releasing their tension or something that will build up their suspense. At every word and every sentence you write you must sense how they are going to take it. Of course it is impossible to do that; but it must at least be attempted. If your imagination is not up to the production of *some* sort of feedback, you are lost.

Dr. Wiener in his book tells of the fascinating fact that a disorder of the feedback produces a certain type of neurosis in human beings, called "purpose tremor"—and that automatic machines, when *their* feedback mechanism breaks down, *develop exactly the same symptoms.* The feedback, in other words, is so basic that lack of it will make you ill.

Does this mean that if you keep on writing without feedback it will eventually make you ill? Yes. There is evidence that if you continue, year after year, to write without renewing direct contact with your readers, it will make you more and more neurotic. In the end, you may not even be able to perform properly the simplest jobs of ordinary communication. Witness this story about Henry James, who spent his whole literary life completely disregarding his readers. Once, when he and Edith Wharton went for an automobile ride, they lost their way and James called over an old man to ask directions. This is what James said:

"My good man, if you'll be good enough to come here, please; a little nearer—so— . . . My friend, to put it to you in two words, this lady and I have just arrived here from Slough; that is to say, to be more strictly accurate, we have recently *passed through* Slough on our way here, having actually motored to Windsor from Rye, which was our point of departure; and the darkness having overtaken us, we should be much obliged if you would tell us where we are now in relation to High Street, which, as you of course know, leads to the Castle, after leaving on the left hand the turn down to the railway station."

The old man didn't answer but looked dazed. So James went on: "In short, my good man, what I want to put to you in a word is this: supposing we have already (as I have reason to think we have) driven past the turn down to the railway station (which, in that case, by the way, would probably not have been on our left hand, but on our right), where are we now in relation to . . ."

At this point Edith Wharton broke in: "Oh please, do ask him where King's Road is."

"Ah—? King's Road? Just so! Quite right! Can you, as a matter of fact, my good man, tell us where, in relation to our present position, King's Road exactly *is*?"

"Ye're on it," the old man said.

Edith Wharton, who told this story in her book *Looking Backward,* of course didn't think of it as an example of neurosis caused by prolonged lack of feedback; but it seems perfectly legitimate to interpret it this way. Henry James wrote so many novels in his involved mandarin style, light-years removed from the ordinary daily speech of human beings, that he finally was unable to talk any other way; instead of the oscillation mentioned by Dr. Wiener, he developed a sort of paralysis of his syntax.

The same sort of thing happens all around us every day: scientists get so wrapped up in their special terminology that they become literally unable to talk standard English; lawyers cannot remember the common-language equivalents of *compensation, consideration,* or *incompetent*; advertising copywriters begin to use expressions like "breakfast discovery" or "less filling" in ordinary conversation.

Some time ago I came into possession of a letter that illustrates strikingly the fossilizing effect of the lack of feedback. This is a case where the disregard of the audience isn't involuntary or neurotic, but deliberate and a matter of policy. How is that possible, you say? Very simple: Imagine a government agency whose business it is to enforce a certain set of regulations. Suppose letters come in asking for exceptions or at least sympathetic interpretations. The best way, obviously, to produce a satisfyingly negative answer is to utterly ignore that feedback information and simply, parrot-like, repeat the words of the regulations.

The document I am speaking of happens to be the answer to a letter from a World War II veteran fighting again in the Korean War. He wanted to take a course under the G.I. Education Bill, but knew there was a July 25, 1951, deadline for starting the training. He couldn't make that deadline since he was busy in Korea fighting another war. So he wrote to the Veterans Administration in Washington asking for an extension. Back came the following answer:

> This is in response to your recent letter concerning education or training under the provisions of Title II of the Servicemen's Readjustment Act of 1944, as amended.
>
> As you know, Title II, Public Law 346, 78th Congress, as amended by Public Law 268, 79th Congress, provides in pertinent part as follows: ". . . That such course shall be initiated not later than <u>four years after either the date of his discharge or the termination of the present war, which-ever is the later. . . ."</u> [Underscoring supplied.]
>
> You will observe from the text of the statutory proviso quoted, that an eligible veteran who wishes to pursue edu-

cation or training thereunder is required to initiate his course as a beneficiary under the law not later than four years after either the date of his discharge or separation from active military or naval service or the termination of World War II, whichever is the later; and this is determined to mean that he must have commenced and be actually pursuing his course as of such date, except for normal interruptions, that is, for summer vacations or other reasons beyond the veteran's control. The statutory proviso quoted constitutes a specific prohibition, the effect of which is to set a specific time limit beyond which veterans may not initiate courses of education or training as beneficiaries under the cited legislation.

It has been determined administratively that any veteran who has timely initiated his course of education or training (other than correspondence study alone) as a beneficiary under the above-referenced legislation prior or subsequent to re-entrance into active military or naval service, whose conduct and progress in such course has been satisfactory, and who is prevented from continuing his course because of an assigned military duty and/or military transfer from place of training will be considered to have interrupted training for a reason or reasons beyond his control. A veteran so circumstanced will be permitted to resume education or training under the law within a reasonable period of time following his release from active military or naval service, notwithstanding the fact that such release may occur subsequent to July 25, 1951—the "deadline date" applicable to his case. It is desired to emphasize, however, that education or training so resumed is limited to the extent of an individual's remaining period of en-

titlement and by the statutory proviso which specifically
stipulates that education or training will not be afforded
beyond July 25, 1956. However, in the case of a person
who voluntarily enlisted or re-enlisted in the Regular Army,
Navy, or Air Force between October 6, 1945—October 5,
1946; that is to say, under the provisions of Section II (a),
Public Law 190, 79th Congress (the Armed Forces Voluntary Recruitment Act of 1945), education or training will
be made available for a 9-year period subsequent to the
veteran's discharge or release from such enlistment or re-
enlistment.

You will observe from the expressions contained in this
communication that continued education or training under
the law subsequent to July 25, 1951 or a date four years
from the date of a veteran's first discharge or release from
active World War II service, if such discharge or release
occurs subsequent to the official termination of World
War II; that is, to say, July 25, 1947, will depend entirely
upon a timely initiation of a course as provided by law.

Possibly you had some difficulty in understanding this letter, so I'll translate it into English. The translation reads as
follows:

"No."

I am gladly willing to admit that this sort of thing is the
exception rather than the rule in our society. The studied disregard of feedback information is mostly confined to government officials, bank and insurance employees with a certain
amount of seniority, and the latter-day disciples of Henry
James.

The rest of us are painfully conscious of the problem; in

fact, it bedevils us day and night. How can we communicate with people and tell them what they want to know? How can we write and know whether we are understood? How can we figure out what's in people's minds if they are not there to tell us? How can we plan beforehand *any* kind of communication if it's true that the principle of the feedback makes all communication unpredictable? How can we consciously prepare for the mysterious mental give-and-take that takes place unconsciously, from moment to moment, haphazardly and unforeseeably?

We can't. And still we must forever try, mountains of paper must be duly covered with writing, communication without feedback must forever be attempted; we must do the best possible job. If we can't see how people react, we must imagine how they *would* react; if we can't do that either we must remember how they *did* react, or guess how they *might* react, or—how about that?—see to it that they *will* react the way we expect them to.

And there we get into very deep waters. For since our society is based on written, planned communication, the problem of the feedback has become one of the basic problems of our way of life; and instead of the true article—the real or imagined face-to-face feedback—we have long ago begun to use an imitation: we have gone in for "second-hand feedback" and finally for "artificial feedback." Let me explain what I mean by these terms.

By "second-hand feedback" I mean a situation where—if you remember Dr. Wiener's definition—we watch the results of *someone else's* behavior to change or regulate our own. Instead of controlling our furnace by the thermostat in our own living room, we hitch it up to the neighbors'. So, if it's tropical in our own living room but freezing at the neighbors', our furnace still keeps going full blast, making us even more uncomfortable than we were before.

You say this is so stupid it can't happen? It happens all the time. Club & Diamond come out with a novel dojiehunkus that sells like hot cakes and arouses enthusiastic feedback cries for more; so, four months later, Heart & Spade are on the market with a practically indistinguishable dojiehunkus in green plastic, selling for twenty-six cents less; another two months, and there is Notrump, Inc. with exactly the same thing, only it makes a noise and sells for under a dollar. Do they succeed? No. It's the second-hand feedback that's wrong. By the time they get around to "modifying their behavior," the season has changed, the public is tired of dojiehunkuses, everybody who wants one already has one, or the new ones are simply so inexpensive that they can't possibly be any good. Who knows? Who can tell what's wrong once the golden moment of immediate communication has passed? Second-hand feedback is an outstanding characteristic of the American system of free enterprise, but that doesn't mean that it always works. The simple truth is that only the real thing is the real thing.

Back in 1944 Leo McCarey directed the movie *Going My Way*, with Bing Crosby, Barry Fitzgerald, and Frank McHugh. That was an example of the real thing. McCarey, as Bing Crosby tells it, "had his own movie-making system. . . . We never knew what we'd be doing from morning to afternoon. We'd come on the set about nine, have coffee and doughnuts, and Leo would go over to a piano and play for a while, while the rest of us sang a little barbershop. Then he'd wander around and think. He might even take a walk down the street and come back, while we waited. About eleven o'clock he'd say, 'Well, let's get going.'

"We'd run through the scene he'd described to us the previous night. Then he'd say, 'We're not going to do that. Take a two-hour lunch break. I'll whip something up and we'll shoot it after lunch.'

"When we came back, what he'd whipped up might change the whole direction of our story. We shot it anyhow."

Going My Way won all sorts of awards and was a terrific box-office success. So immediately half a dozen other films were made showing happy-go-lucky Catholic priests or nuns engaged in unorthodox antics. Did they succeed? No. They imitated the external, visible features of *Going My Way* as closely as possible, but how could anyone imitate Leo McCarey's method of picture-making? You can't plan a repetition of the unpredictable. You can't rely on second-hand feedback. You can't cash in on someone else's success.

And what do I mean by "artificial feedback"? Just this: If you are interested, and in a position to do so, you can arrange things so that your audience will feed back to you exactly the response you want to hear. That won't give you any clue as to their true state of mind, to be sure, but it will give you something to work with and that's often extremely useful. The simplest and most innocuous example of this is the "Give the little girl a great big hand" type of thing; the most elaborate and sinister is the "spontaneous" *Sieg—Heil!* in Nazi mass meetings or the "voluntary" confessions in Communist treason trials. In between there are all sorts of dubious and disturbing situations, and it's not always easy to figure out where to draw the line between the harmless and dangerous. For where does the legitimate selling of ideas and products end and where does the misleading creation of a response begin? We Americans, through the successful efforts of advertising, have been stimulated to demand a new car every year, king-size cigarettes, lighter beer and sugar-coated cereals. Would we have raised these demands spontaneously? If not, is this "artificial feedback" good or bad? Is our economy a fool's paradise that will one day crash down about our ears, or is the creation of new demands the road to progress?

One thing is sure: If you rely on an artificially created response to decide what to do or say, you are on slippery ground. Like the wife who has made her husband tell her every day that he loves her, you will after a while begin to doubt the sincerity of that gratifying response. Only the immediate, the unpredictable is worth listening to.

And now let's look at some situations where the feedback was used properly and intelligently. After all, there *are* sensible people who don't need to be told that genuine response is what counts. One of those sensible people is Mr. Stanley L. Payne, a market and public opinion researcher who wrote a highly interesting book on *The Art of Asking Questions* (Princeton University Press, 1951). The feedback taught Mr. Payne some surprising and enlightening things. Is "correct grammar," for instance, an advantage in finding the truth? Mr. Payne learned that it is not. People are more likely to answer sincerely if they are asked "ungrammatical" questions, like "Which are the most courteous—the salesmen or the repairmen?"

Or does it matter in what order you state an alternative for people to choose from? Logically it doesn't, but psychologically it certainly does, as Mr. Payne discovered by comparing his feedback answers. He asked a group of people: "Do you think of the oil industry as being owned by thousands of small stockholders or by a few large investors?" Then he asked another group: "Do you think of the oil industry as being owned by a few large investors or by thousands of small stockholders?" Did the percentage figures of the two sets of answers match? They did not. It turned out that about 7 percent of all people will simply echo the words they heard *last*. (Which confirms the old rule of rhetoric that the place for emphasis is at the end.)

The advertising profession also has members who are willing to accept humbly whatever lessons they can derive from genuine feedback response. Mostly they are men who have gone through the hard school of mail-order and coupon advertising. For it is possible to theorize prettily—and quite misleadingly—about the effect of institutional ads and the value of television shows; but when it comes to counting how many people have sent in coupons, you are up against the facts of life. Which is why the study of mail-order and coupon advertising gets you down to the bedrock of effective communication.

The best book on the subject is *Tested Advertising Methods* by John Caples, which was published first in 1932 (by Harper & Brothers) and is still just as good as it was twenty years ago—filled to the brim with hard, incontrovertible facts. Among those facts are the following rules for writing successful mail-order ads—rules that apply just as well to any other kind of communication:

1. Use the present tense, second person. (E.g. You are reading these words now in my book. Remember them!)

2. Choose simple words.

3. Give free information. (E.g. I just told you about Mr. Caples' excellent book.)

4. Arouse curiosity. (E.g. My next chapter is called "Poor Man's Psychoanalysis." Aren't you curious what it's going to be about?)

5. Make your copy specific.

6. Use long copy. (The mail-order people know, as a hard fact, that you can't be stingy with words if you want to make an impression. Brevity is a virtue—in theory; in practice, when it comes to selling things, or persuading people to do things, or teaching people, you have to be lavish with words. Go into details; explain everything that *may* need an explanation; give examples; paraphrase; repeat; let the words flow as long as you are reasonably sure they will be read or listened to. Exert yourself. If you can condense your whole message into one short sentence, don't. Use thirty sentences, filled with stuff worth hearing or reading.)

7. Urge the reader to act. (E.g. Take a pencil and copy these seven rules of Mr. Caples'. They are worth their weight in gold.)

Of course I don't mean to say that only the mail-order people know how to write advertising copy. There are many other copywriters who have an instinct for feedback and write consumers' English rather than Madison Avenue patois. One of these is Mr. Leslie Pearl who writes the ads for Wallachs men's stores in New York City. Here is a recent example of his work, exemplifying beautifully all of Mr. Caples' seven points:

BON VOYAGE

Phil Lerman, manager of the Wallachs store in Newark, got a phone call at his home at seven o'clock in the morning one day last week. It was a young man who had purchased some slacks, arranged to call for them, and then forgotten to do so. Now he was sailing for Europe at ten-thirty. Our store wouldn't open in time for him to get his parcel and get to the pier on time.

Mr. Lerman got dressed fast, went downtown, opened up the store and found the slacks. As he tied the box he asked the young man how he had located his home phone number without even knowing his name. "That was easy," he replied, "I just asked the police."

All of which brings us to our point which is that any man going to Europe for a vacation should make Wallachs his first port of call. We have everything you'll need for wearing on board, boulevard or beach. We can outfit you smartly, expeditiously and economically.

My favorite example of the feedback principle does not come from advertising, though. It's a book—a whole book filled with advice on how to speak and write, based solely on the actual live response from real audiences. The book is called *How to Write a Speech* (McGraw-Hill, 1951); its author is Mr. Edward J. Hegarty, who has been training salesmen of the Westinghouse Electric Corporation for some twenty-five or thirty years. Finally, on the basis of his enormous experience in talking to ordinary Americans so that they will understand and remember, Mr. Hegarty wrote his book. Ostensibly it tells you how to write a speech—primarily a speech addressed to a sales meeting; actually, it contains just about everything anyone needs to know about effective speaking and writing for all practical purposes I can possibly imagine. You can follow Mr. Hegarty's advice and write an excellent paper on nuclear physics; you can use it to make a campaign

speech for the United States Senate; or you can get help from
it on how to write a letter to your mother-in-law. In short, I
firmly believe that Mr. Hegarty's book is just about the best
practical English textbook in existence; reading it will do you
more good than studying two dozen garden-variety college or
high school texts. It's as if the geography of Afghanistan were
a required subject in all our schools: the textbook writers
got their stuff in the library, but Mr. Hegarty was *there*.

This is Hegarty on How to Write:

> The shoes you are wearing, the pants that show the
> shine, the hat that cries aloud for cleaning—all such things
> can be brought into the speech in a way that will create in-
> terest in the audience. For these are the things those people
> out front know. One man's hat needs cleaning, another's
> shoes need new heels. When you talk about these things,
> you are one of them.

> Tell how the Missus plays bridge even though she has
> taken all those lessons. Explain how your sister-in-law won't
> let her husband sit in the white chair. Then talk about the
> mean aunt who won't allow any dogs in the house. Your
> boy of high-school age and his high opinion of you always
> brings a smile to the faces of the listeners. They have kids
> with similar lofty opinions.

> The peeves of any audience are good talk material. A
> speaker tells you how his wife insists on lighting the din-
> ner table with candles. Most men in the audience go
> through the same ordeal whenever they have company.
> With a wonderful invention like the electric light, women
> insist on eating by candlelight. Now that is good speech

material. I have heard it used. Lipstick on water-cooler bubblers is another good peeve that gets the men. Ah, yes, there are lots of them.

If you wanted to make the point that most automobiles in the country are ten years old, make the statement, then ask, "How old is yours?"

If you wear a toupee, talk about that. Did you ever hear a fellow who wore a toupee mention it? Not so you can notice it. But wouldn't such a mention keep the audience awake?

Hegarty's *How to Write a Speech* is, as I said, the best example of the feedback principle that I know of. For when you read the book you don't really learn anything from Mr. Hegarty himself; you learn solely what all those audiences have taught *him*. It's the pure metal of actual audience response, refined for you to use and apply. Without the feedback neither Mr. Hegarty nor you nor anyone else would ever think of talking to an audience about lipstick on water-cooler bubblers or about a toupee; but if you expose yourself to enough audiences you will learn that these things communicate ideas, while expressions like "the gradient of the socio-economic differential" do not.

And why don't they? Again because of the feedback. Only this time it's a negative feedback. The same audience that will laugh, prick up their ears and pay close attention as soon as you start talking about your toupee—that same audience will grow restless, cough, and wiggle in their seats at the sound of "gradients of the socio-economic differential." They will feed you back information all right, but information that your words have not registered, that you'd better lay off that fancy vocabulary of yours, that they want to hear more about your toupee and about your Uncle Julius who would always hurry to the depot at 6 A.M. when he had to make an eight oclock train. The mathematicians have a name for that kind of negative feedback; it's an interesting and suggestive name. They call it "semantic noise."

To explain the term, I have to tell you something about the mathematical theory of communication, which is the brainchild of Dr. Claude Shannon of the Bell Telephone Laboratories. Dr. Shannon worked out a theoretical formula for the amount of information you can get through a channel of communication—say, a telephone connection. The formula works perfectly only for a noiseless channel; as soon as there is any noise, the amount of information that can be communicated is cut down. However, there may be a "redundancy" in the way the information is transmitted: the message may contain more material than is actually necessary to convey the information. If so, "redundancy will help combat noise," as Dr. Shannon says. In other words, a seemingly unnecessary repetition in the message may be useful because it will counteract the obstacle of noise. (If there is a buzz in the telephone, you have to say things twice.)

Now this whole theory can also be applied to the *mental* aspects of communication, and you can use the term "semantic noise" for anything that interferes with the recipient's "getting" the message mentally—unfamiliar vocabulary, dull delivery, difficulty of the subject matter, overcondensation, or lack of interest in general. To counteract that "semantic noise" you have to use redundancy. If they don't get it, you have to repeat.

For example, suppose you call Schnickelfritz & Co. and

you say, "This is Mr. Silas Marner. Can I talk to Mr. Schnick-elfritz?"

"Mr. Sinus Warner?" you hear. "Just a moment, please."

"No," you say. "Mr. *Silas Marner.*"

"Pardon me, sir. Mr. Midas Barber? Just a moment."

"No," you say. "*Silas Marner*—ess eye el aye ess, em aye are en ee are."

"Oh, excuse me; Mr. Virus Parker. I'll have Mr. Schnickel-fritz for you in a minute."

"No," you say, "the name is *Silas Marner*—ess as in slow-witted, eye as in inefficient, el as in low I.Q. . ."

And so on. The greater the semantic noise, the more re-dundancy is necessary. You have to modify your behavior ac-cording to the feedback. As long as your message doesn't get through, you have to repeat, expand, embroider, illustrate, go over the material again and again.

This is one of the great "secrets" of all speaking and writ-ing. Semantic noise is everywhere, and often it's deafening. People don't pay any attention to what you say, their thoughts wander, they are tired, they are bored, they are interested in something else, they have doctor bills, their wives are unfaith-ful to them, they don't like the suit you are wearing or the jacket of your book, they suddenly remember a funny story they heard yesterday, or they just fall asleep. Nothing but semantic noise and there you are, trying to tell them some-thing. Without the help of redundancy you might as well give up.

Most people don't realize that great truth. They are deaf to semantic noise. They write, or prepare their speeches, in ut-ter solitude—way off somewhere in a semantically soundproof ivory tower. Inside their heads you could hear a pin drop.

Everything is quiet, wonderfully peaceful and quiet, and all thoughts reach their destination without the slightest obstacle. No sooner are things said and put down on paper than they are communicated to the audience. In the never-never land without semantic noise nothing needs to be said more than once.

In reality, it's the other way round. Most things have to be repeated seventeen times, like the theme of Ravel's *Bolero*. Or you have to think up twenty variations upon your theme, as Shakespeare did when he wrote the famous speech in *Richard II* about "this blessed plot, this earth, this realm, this England."

You don't believe in redundancy? Read the Bible. Read the twenty-fourth and twenty-fifth chapters of the Gospel of St. Matthew, in which Jesus preaches the lesson, "Watch, for ye know not what hour your Lord doth come." First he compares the coming of the Lord to the flood that came suddenly in the days of Noah; then he tells the parable of the thief; then that of the wicked servant; then that of the foolish virgins; then that of the buried talent; and finally he talks about the sheep and the goats, repeating the main lesson: "Inasmuch as ye have done it unto one of the least of my brethren, ye have done it unto me."

In the two thousand years that have passed since, that lesson has been preached millions of times—a redundancy made necessary by tremendous semantic noise.

No, don't disparage redundancy: it's the only weapon you have against the semantic noise that surrounds you. You say you believe in what you are saying? You say you have already repeated it five times? Go ahead: say it twenty times more in twenty different ways. Maybe then someone will begin to catch on.

8
Poor Man's Psychoanalysis

*One has information only to the extent to which
one has tended to communicate one's experience.*
—HARRY STACK SULLIVAN

EVERYBODY KNOWS BY NOW, MORE OR LESS,
what it's like to go to a psychoanalyst. You
go to his office; he asks you to lie down on a couch; then he
sits down behind you with a notebook; then he asks you to
talk. You talk and talk and talk—you say aloud everything
that comes to your mind. You talk about yourself, your
troubles, your worries, what happened during the day, what
you ate for lunch, a silly joke someone told you, what this
reminds you of, what you dreamed during the night, where
you spent the summer when you were five years old, what
was your father's favorite dish, the time when you went digging for crawfish at night with flashlights, how you frightened
your mother by bringing home a dead mouse, your thoughts
about sex, more thoughts about sex, still more thoughts about
sex, why you married your wife and why you didn't marry
that other girl twelve years ago— . . . and so on and on and

on, talk, talk, talk, the bubbles that come to the surface of your mind, endlessly.

That's the method; that's the famous therapy that you have read about, that you have seen made fun of in dozens of magazine cartoons; the technique that has made more of a stir than practically anything that has ever happened in the history of medicine.

Did you ever ask yourself where it all came from? How on earth did anyone ever think of such an extraordinary business? How did this fantastic method spring from the mind of Sigmund Freud in the first place? Did he experiment with it and suddenly discover that it worked? Or did he read about it in a book? If so, in what book? Was it a technique practiced by some doctor before him? Or did he adapt it from something else? What exactly happened when the famous "free association" method appeared for the first time in history?

I did ask myself these questions, and I found the answer. The story is a little involved, but if you bear with me, you'll find it interesting. (And pertinent to this book, as you'll see.)

Freud, as many people know, started his work by treating patients under hypnosis. Then, in the late 1890's, he found hypnosis more and more unsatisfactory and began to look around for a substitute. He remembered from his student days how a professor had gotten information from patients *without* hypnosis by simply giving them a lot of encouragement to talk. This started Freud thinking. In his autobiography he writes: "My patients, I reflected, must in fact 'know' all the things which had hitherto only been made accessible to them in hypnosis: and assurances and encouragement on my part, assisted perhaps by the touch of my hand, would, I thought, have the power of forcing the forgotten facts and connections into consciousness." And so Freud abandoned hypnosis and started treating his patients with the technique of "encouraged" free talk.

But that wasn't yet the "free association" method that we know today. In fact, it was rather the opposite: instead of leaving the patient to his own devices on what to talk about, the psychiatrist took a hand and helped. So there was a second switch from "encouraged" talk to the absolutely free talk that is the really essential feature of the psychoanalytical method. That second switch occurred in 1898 when Freud was treating a hysterical young girl by name of Dora. (Her case history is now a famous medical classic.) Dora was the first person in history who was treated by "free association."

And how did Freud finally hit on that method? In his autobiography, oddly enough, he didn't say. However, he did write a short paper in 1920, entitled *A Note on the Pre-History of the Technique of Analysis*. And there he told the story.

Freud wrote his paper in answer to a book by Havelock Ellis, called *The Philosophy of Conflict*. In that book Ellis has written the following:

In 1857, Dr. J. Garth Wilkinson, more noted as a Swedenborgian mystic and poet than as a physician, published a volume of mystic doggerel verse written by what he considered "a new method," the method of "Impression." "A theme is chosen and written down," he stated; "as soon as this is done the first impression upon the mind which succeeds the act of writing the title is the beginning of the evolution of that theme, no matter how strange or alien the word or phrase may seem. . . . The first mental movement, the first word that comes is the response to the mind's

desire for the unfolding of that subject." It is continued by
the same method, and Garth Wilkinson adds: "I have always found it led by an infallible instinct into the subject."
The method was, as Garth Wilkinson viewed it, a kind of
exalted *laissez faire*, a command to the deepest unconscious
instincts to express themselves. Reason and will, he pointed
out, are left aside; you trust to an "influx," and the faculties
of the mind are "directed to ends they know not of." Garth
Wilkinson, it must be clearly understood, although he was
a physician, used this method for religious and literary, and
never for scientific or medical ends; but it is easy to see that
essentially it is the method of psychoanalysis applied to
oneself, and it is further evidence how much Freud's method
is an artist's method.

Did Freud admit that he got the "free association" method
from Garth Wilkinson? Not at all. He had never heard of the
man's name before he read Ellis' book. But—and this is
where we get our answer—but he remembered now (he wrote
in 1920) that there was a similar description in a brief essay
by the German writer Ludwig Börne. He had been a Börne
fan ever since he was fourteen years old; he still kept the volume with Börne's penetrating essay around; in fact, he reread
it from time to time. So he, Freud, was rather inclined to
think that that's where he got the original idea for his method.

This is the only explanation that has ever been offered for
the astonishing invention of the psychoanalytical method.
Since Freud himself said so, we may take it for granted that
it's true. That is, we may consider it an established fact that
*psychoanalysis goes back to a self-analysis technique first de-
scribed by Ludwig Börne*. From which it follows that if you
are unwilling or unable to spend sixty or seventy-five dollars a

week for three years or so on psychoanalytical treatment, you might read and apply Börne's essay and get more or less the same thing for free. The title I gave this chapter, "Poor Man's Psychoanalysis," is not just a figure of speech; I meant it literally. This is it.

When I had read Freud's paper I went to the library and dug up Börne's essay. It was written in 1823 and is called "The Art of Becoming an Original Writer in Three Days." Fortunately it is so short that I can reprint it here in full. Here it is:

There are men and books that teach Latin, Greek or French in three days, and bookkeeping in only three hours. So far, however, no one has offered a course in How to Become a Good Original Writer in Three Days. And yet, it's so easy! There is nothing to learn, but plenty to unlearn; nothing to acquire, but much to forget. The minds and books of today's writers are like those old manuscripts where you first have to scratch off the boring disputations of a church step-father or the mumblings of a monk before you get down to a Roman classic. Every human mind is born with beautiful ideas—new ideas too, since in every human being the world is created anew. But life and education write their useless stuff over them and cover them up.

To see things as they really are, consider this: We know an animal, a fruit, a flower in their true shape; they appear to us the way they are. But would anyone understand the true nature of a chicken, an apple tree, or a rose if he knew only chicken pie, apple sauce, or rose perfume? And yet that's all we ever get in the sciences and in anything that we take in through our minds rather than our senses. It comes to us changed and made over; we never get to know it in its raw, naked form. Thinking is the kitchen where all truths are killed, plucked, cut up, fried, and pickled. What we need most today are *unthinking* books—books with *things* in them rather than thoughts.

There are only very few original writers. Our best writers differ from the poorer ones far less than you might think. One writer creeps to his goal, another runs, a third hobbles, a fourth dances, a fifth drives, a sixth rides on horseback: but the goal and the road are common to all. Great new ideas are found only in solitude: but where is solitude to be found? You can get away from people—and at once you are in the noisy market-place of books; you can throw away the books too; but how do you clear the mind of all the conventional ideas that education has poured into it? The true art of self-training is the art of making yourself ignorant: the finest and most useful of the arts but one that is rarely and poorly practiced. In a million people there are only a thousand thinkers and in a thousand thinkers only one self-thinker. People today are like gruel, kept in shape only by the pot; you find hardness and firmness only in the crust, the lowest layer of the people; and gruel stays gruel— if a golden spoon scoops out a mouthful, it tears relatives apart but does not end relationships.

The true search for knowledge is not like the voyage of Columbus but like that of Ulysses. Man is born abroad, living means seeking your home, and thinking means living. But the home of ideas is the heart; if you want fresh water, you must draw from that source; the mind is but a river, on whose banks live thousands who muddy its waters by washing, bathing, flax-steeping, and other dirty business. The mind is the arm, the heart is the will. Strength can be acquired, increased and trained; but what good is strength without the courage to use it? A cowardly fear of thinking curbs us all; the censorship of public opinion is more oppressive than that of governments. Most writers are no better than they are because they have ideas but no character. Their weakness comes from vanity. They want to surpass their fellow writers; but to surpass someone you must meet him on his own ground, to overtake someone you must travel the same road. That's why good writers have so much in common with bad ones: the good one is like the bad one but a little bigger; he goes in the same direction but a little farther.

To be original you must listen to the voice of your heart rather than the clamor of the world—and have the courage to teach publicly what you have learned. The source of all genius is sincerity; men would be wiser if they were more moral.

And now follows the application that I promised: Take several sheets of paper and for three days in succession, without any pretense or hypocrisy, write down everything that comes to your mind. Write what you think about yourself, about women, about the Turkish War, about Goethe, about the Fonk Trial, about the Last Judgment, about your boss—and after three days you will be beside yourself with surprise at all the new, unheard-of ideas you had. That's the art of becoming an original writer in three days!

Börne's essay is a wonderful piece of writing and thinking. I have reread it many times, and find it almost inexhaustible. Börne was at the height of his powers when he wrote it; it is an outburst of pure genius, written straight from the heart.

But what we are concerned with here is the method—the

famous technique, the original honest-to-goodness source of a large chunk of twentieth-century psychiatry. What exactly is it that Börne says? Very simple: Write down everything that comes to your mind, don't stop, don't shy away from any subject, forget all "pretense and hypocrisy." That's all. Can it be really all? Can it be that this childishly simple procedure will do the same thing for you as prolonged treatment by a highly trained professional psychiatrist? It's hard to believe, I know. I don't expect you to believe it, and I can't present much evidence that it is so. What I do have is a number of facts that have convinced me that Börne's method is well worth trying. Besides—and that's what interests us here—it isn't just a kind of *ersatz* psychoanalysis but an excellent technique for normal people who want to straighten out their minds and improve their thinking.

To begin with, the technique of dredging thoughts up from your unconscious is the oldest literary technique in the world. In fact, once you start to think about it, it is clear that *all* works of literature are more or less produced that way. No writer in the world has ever neatly thought out his poem or short story, with all the adjectives and commas in place, and then sat down to copy faithfully what he had prepared in his mind. It's ridiculous; it doesn't happen. What happens, with everybody from lyrical poet to scholarly historian, is that there is some kind of unformed material in the mind and *in the act of writing* the thought is born. You don't first think and then write; the better you are as a writer, the more professional you are, the more you rely on the process of shaping your thoughts as you go along. All of which corresponds of course exactly to the method of the best speakers: inspired oratory is the child of the moment, born out of the union of speaker and audience.

I can't possibly give you all the evidence on that aspect of writing: there is too much of it. There are libraries full of books containing statements by writers on how they wrote their books. Each one of them, one way or the other, says that he doesn't know just how the words finally got from his mind onto paper. The process is always unconscious. A writer, just like any other artist, is someone who "lets down a bucket into his subconscious," as E. M. Forster called it. Everything that has ever been said about writing or speaking ends in a mystery: we don't have the slightest notion of how words and ideas "come to our minds."

But we don't have to go into that mystery. All we want at the moment is a statement by a writer—or statements by several writers—that they used something like the Börne method and that it worked. We already know the description by Garth Wilkinson, quoted by Havelock Ellis. Are there any parallel statements by others?

For all I know there may be dozens of them, in all of the world's great literary languages. I have found four—four descriptions of a literary technique that roughly parallels that of Börne. All four of them seem to have been independent discoveries.

Exhibit Number One is a letter Thomas Carlyle wrote to his future wife Jane Welsh on December 25, 1822. I quote:

"Sit down and write . . . write and write, though you could swear it was the most stupid stuff in nature. . . . Be not too careful for a subject; take the one you feel most interested in or understand best. . . . And for a commencement, why should it give you pause? Rush forward and fear nothing."

Exhibit Number Two was written by Lafcadio Hearn. Or rather, it was spoken by him since it comes from one of his lectures to Japanese students. Hearn's advice to beginning or aspiring writers was this: "Write down immediately, as fully as you can, the circumstances and the cause of the emotion, and try to describe the feeling as far as possible. It makes no difference then whether you write at all grammatically nor whether you write backwards or forwards. The all-essential thing is to have notes of the experience."

Exhibit Three is a whole book—*Everyman's Genius* by Mary Austin, published in 1923. In that book Mary Austin tells the beginning writer to get himself into a state of mystic contemplation or meditation; only that way ideas will come to him. *Everyman's Genius* is written in the most astonishing special terminology; the process of getting material out of the unconscious is called "autoprayer." Nevertheless, it's quite obvious that what Mary Austin is talking about is exactly the same thing as the method described by Börne, Wilkinson, Carlyle and Lafcadio Hearn.

Finally, there is Exhibit Four: *Becoming a Writer* by Dorothea Brande (Harcourt, Brace & Co., 1934). *Becoming a Writer* is one of the best-known and most successful how-to-write books that have ever been published. Mrs. Brande is highly specific in her advice—too specific for my own taste, I should say. Again, this is a book of directions on how to get your unconscious into operation. Here is what you are told to do: First, "learn to hold your mind as still as your body." (This is all right; in fact, the main secret of putting your unconscious to work is to *stop thinking*.) But then Mrs. Brande goes on: Focus your attention on something like a child's gray rubber ball; then "close your eyes and go on looking at the ball, thinking of nothing else." When you have trained yourself to do that, you are ready for the real stuff. It goes like this: 1. Think of your story or whatever it is you want to write. 2. Go for a walk. 3. Take a bath. 4. Go into a dim room and lie down flat on your back. 5. Wait for the "artistic coma"; and 6. Bingo! Here it comes: "You will feel a definite impulse to rise, a kind of surge of energy. Obey it at once; you will be in a slightly somnambulistic state indifferent to everything on earth except what you are about to write; dull to all the outer world but vividly alive to the world of your imagination. Get up and go to your paper or typewriter, and begin to write."

Well, I don't know. That sort of thing may be all right for some people, but as for me, this is where I stopped my researches in the literary and how-to-write field. The natural next question I asked myself was this: What about the psychiatrists? Hasn't any one of *them* discovered the Börne method or something like it? Of course a psychiatrist will hardly send a patient home and tell him to cure himself; nevertheless, there must be *some* scientifically-minded people who played around with the self-analysis idea. Where were they?

That one was easy. First, there is a book by Karen Horney called *Self-Analysis*, which shows how a patient can continue an analysis alone, having "free association" sessions by himself and taking notes of everything that comes to his mind. Second, there is *Victory Over Fear* by Professor John Dollard of Yale, containing a slightly different technique of a more conscious, deliberate written self-analysis. (Professor Dollard calls this "self-study.") However, neither of those books is very helpful for the person who wants to know exactly what to do and how to do it. The ideal book for that purpose is *Analyze Yourself* by E. Pickworth Farrow.

The interesting thing about the Farrow book is that he is not a psychiatrist but an ex-patient. (He is a doctor of science, not of medicine.) His book is called *Analyze Yourself—Enabling Anyone to Become Deeply Psycho-Analyzed Without a Personal Analyst* (International Universities Press, 1945). There is a brief foreword by no less a sponsor than Sigmund Freud himself, who explicitly endorses Farrow's method and says that he has used it himself to analyze his own dreams.

As Dr. Farrow tells it, he had undergone treatment by two analysts, but finally got fed up with both of them. So he went home and decided to do the job himself. How? By the Börne method, of course—rediscovered independently for the umptieth time. Dr. Farrow set aside an hour each day, laid in a large supply of paper, picked an easy pen that wouldn't play him any tricks, and proceeded with the self-treatment. His description of his method is worth reading: "One must *write down on the paper whatever comes into one's conscious mind at any given instant*—and this, in fact, is the great key to the method. If it occurs to one that this method is silly—write this down. If it occurs to one that it is a waste of time—write this down. If it occurs to one that one would like to be deeply analyzed and wonders if one has some particular complex, but is quite sure that this method will never discover it—very well, write this down." To which Dr. Farrow adds that if there are several thoughts that come to mind, the one *most insistent* ought to be written down. If your mind is a blank, write down "My mind is now a blank." And don't try to get around the writing by using a dictating machine; Dr. Farrow tried that and it didn't work. It made him feel like dictating to himself rather than listening to his unconscious.

And that's it. There is no doubt that the Börne method works. It has been used by Dr. Farrow, by Dr. Horney's patients, by Professor Dollard's students, and by an uncounted number of writers and would-be writers. It is a tested, perfectly reliable tool to put your thoughts in shape.

Let me repeat, I am not telling you that you are a neurotic and ought to apply some substitute psychiatry to yourself. I simply say that this self-analysis method is a handy way to clear your mind whenever you feel it needs clearing. To sum it up in my own words, the method consists in this:

Write down everything that comes to your mind. Don't think about what you write; concentrate on putting down as many words as possible. Don't pause in your writing; every thought in your mind should get down on paper. Don't hesitate to put down what is trivial, silly, indecent, irrelevant, or unacceptable. Simply take dictation from your unconscious. Listen to what it says and put down every word.

You may say that this method of writing is the exact opposite of what I recommended to you in Chapter 5. There I told you to do legwork, to keep your eyes open, to take notes on what's going on around you. Now I am telling you to retire to a room where you are undisturbed, to sit down and listen to yourself, to take notes on what's going on inside your mind. Am I blowing hot and cold? Am I telling you to be an introvert and an extravert at the same time?

I know this looks utterly inconsistent. But I can't help that. To write and speak well—to make sense—you have to live fully in both worlds, the outer and the inner. You have to have experience first, as much experience as possible, facts, pictures, events that fill your mind. Then, after you have done your work in taking notes or at least observing and learning, you ought to *forget* all that you have learned. Let it sink down into your unconscious, it's the only place where it will do you any good. And then, when the moment of communication is here—to an audience or at least to yourself—pour it out without thinking, pull it up again from your unconscious by the act of writing and speaking, and you will have something that you can communicate successfully. Otherwise—if you collect material and then laboriously reproduce that material for your listeners or readers—you haven't contributed anything in the process: you are just a parrot or a phonograph. There won't be any life in what you say or write, because you haven't *given* it any life. You were afraid: you didn't have the courage to let it go, drop it into your unconscious and get it up again when you needed it. You didn't trust your own powers before an audience or before a blank sheet of paper. So you stutter and stumble; you hesitate; you erase; you correct; you qualify; you shrink back from revealing what is really on your mind. The result is failure. The facts are there; the grammar, the vocabulary, the syntax, the punctuation; but the vital something is missing. Without using your unconscious you can't communicate.

The Börne method is therefore wonderful training for people who are afraid to let themselves go. You are alone with yourself; you can destroy everything you write if you feel like it; nothing stands in the way of your opening your mind wide. Let it all come out. The real trouble with writing and speaking is timidity; we are all cowards before an audience and stutterers on paper. Write down whatever crosses your mind;

here is your golden chance to speak up bravely and unafraid. (This is much harder than it looks; most of us are afraid of even a private meeting with the truth.)

One thing more: The method works best in the morning. Most professional writers are at their desks early in the morning. Sleep lowers the barriers between the conscious and the unconscious; so morning is the time to go fishing in the depths of your mind. The ultimate recipe for making sense is this: know the facts; forget them and sleep; wake up and write or speak.

But is that all that is to be said? Do we have to accept the facts without wondering about what's behind them? Are we supposed to let down buckets into our own unconscious without curiosity about the source of our inner wealth? No. We can't just let the matter go at this point. It would be inhuman not to speculate on the tremendous mystery of the mind.

Where do our unconscious thoughts come from? Freud answered that they were childhood memories and other painful experiences that had been repressed; to him, the main contents of the unconscious were unwelcome ideas of sex, pain, frustration, unfulfilled desires, shocks.

But much time has gone by since the days of Freud, and modern psychiatrists think differently. There are good things in the unconscious too, they say. Deep down we are not only lustful animals but also rational, intelligent human beings. Says Dr. Erich Fromm, speaking of dreams: "We are not only less reasonable and less decent in our dreams but we are also more intelligent, wiser, and capable of better judgment when we are asleep than when we are awake." Similarly, Dr. O. H. Mowrer thinks that neurotics suffer from repressed morality. And Dr. Viktor Frankl of Vienna, leader of the newest school of "existential analysis," writes of "God in the unconscious," proclaiming that the ultimate source of mental troubles is the repression of our unconscious faith in God.

And so the latest thought in psychiatry leads straight back to Börne ("Every human mind is born with beautiful ideas") and even further back to Socrates. For it is in Plato's Socratic dialogue *Meno* that we first read: "As all nature is akin, and the soul has learned all things, there is no difficulty in her eliciting, or as men say learning, all out of a single recollection, if a man is strenuous and does not faint; for all inquiry and all learning is but recollection." What does that mean? It means that Socrates' theory was exactly what we are after here: he taught that the unconscious is an inexhaustible source of ideas and all learning consists in recalling what we have forgotten.

This may seem fantastic and incredible but there is no doubt that Socrates believed in it fully. In the same Platonic dialogue, *Meno*, Socrates proves his theory by a demonstration. He calls an ignorant slave boy and by skillful questioning makes him produce the solution to a difficult geometrical problem. How could the boy do that? Just so, says Socrates: "He had this knowledge in him. . . . Without any one teaching him he will recover this knowledge for himself, if he is only asked questions."

Not many people today believe in the Socratic theory of the mind. They pay lip service to the "Socratic method," thinking that it consists in having a little discussion after each lecture. But it consists in much more: it consists in having Socrates' own, complete faith in the soul's knowledge of all things. Only a teacher who really believes this is able to ask questions without immediately trying to answer them himself. Only such a teacher trusts the minds of his students to arrive at knowledge and truth under their own power. If the unconscious can't be expected to furnish the right answers, then the teacher or the textbook must supply them, and all talk about using the Socratic method remains just talk; but if the Socratic theory is really applied, students are taught in a way they will never forget.

True Socratic teachers are rare, but they are not an extinct race. One of them was the late Professor Horace Williams who taught logic and philosophy at the University of North Carolina and made an indelible impression on all his students. Another is Professor Nathaniel Cantor, who taught a Socratic course on criminology at the University of Buffalo and later wrote a book about it, called *Dynamics of Learning*. In the book he quotes one of his students:

> I feel that you, as a professor, have contributed more to me than any other teacher with whom I have ever come in contact. The reason for this feeling is that we are ourselves in this class. We are living. We are not spending an hour of having someone else live for us. We are not stuffed with concepts and ideologies which take on no meaning to us. The material, which could easily be lectured to us in very abstract terms, is discussed by all of us, in a very human, natural way. I have learned not to be afraid to listen to those who disagree and not to be afraid to express myself.

And so I think that the Socratic theory is right. It works—not only in the *Dialogues* of Plato but also in Chapel Hill, North Carolina, and in Buffalo, New York. If you apply the Socratic method of teaching or the Börne method of writing to bring ideas up from the unconscious, you tap an inexhaustible source.

Is this mysticism? Perhaps. Perhaps it is religion. For the Börne method of writing is also akin to all prayer, all meditation, all mystic recollection. Mystics don't usually write down the thoughts that come to them during meditation, but sometimes they do. One of the newest religious movements, the Oxford Group, makes this even a regular practice. Observers have often ridiculed the Oxford Group "Quiet Time" with their curious habit of jotting down the particulars of divine guidance in a little notebook. But it's not so easy to make fun of these things when one remembers that the Oxford Group brought forth Alcoholics Anonymous, a movement that has helped hundreds of thousands to regain their mental and physical health.

And then there are always the Quakers—perfectly respectable people who live right among us and openly, unashamedly rely on the Inner Light to guide their actions. A Quaker doesn't need the Börne method because he has been doing that sort of thing habitually ever since childhood. The Quaker religion consists simply in listening to the voice within and in doing what it says. Socrates said, "The soul has learned all things. . . . All learning is but recollection." Quakers prefer the way the same idea is phrased in the Fourteenth Chapter of the Gospel of St. John: "But the Comforter, which is the Holy Ghost, whom the Father will send in my name, he shall teach you all things."

And this is where all speculation ends. All I can say is, Try this method; it works; it will lead you to unsuspected discoveries. I have used it. I have found that it is particularly helpful at the point where you have collected all the material for a speech or a piece of writing and don't know how to organize it. Think about your subject and pour out as many words about it as you can. (Use pencil, pen, or typewriter, whatever is easiest for you; write longhand, shorthand, or abbreviate wildly as you go along.) Do this for half an hour. At the end of the half-hour your speech or article will have organized itself with a beginning, a middle, and an end—and you will have a large number of new ideas that came to you mysteriously and asked to be written down.

You don't have to believe me; you can test the method tomorrow morning. You'll find that I am right—or, as Socrates would have said, you will then remember what you have really known all the time.

9
How to Talk to Anybody

Walk through life and talk to anybody.
—Persian proverb

T HERE IS AN UNFORGETTABLE SCENE IN *Lust for Life,* Irving Stone's famous novel about the life of Vincent Van Gogh. Shortly after Van Gogh arrives in Paris, he goes to an exhibition and sees for the first time paintings of the new Impressionist school. He is overwhelmed. Degas, Monet, Manet, and all the rest—their pictures are a revelation to him.

From the age of twelve he had been used to seeing dark and sombre paintings; paintings in which the brushwork was invisible, every detail of the canvas correct and complete, and flat colors shaded slowly into each other. . . . The paintings that laughed at him merrily from the walls were like nothing he had ever seen or dreamed of. Gone were the flat, thin surfaces. Gone was the sentimental sobriety. Gone was the brown gravy in which Europe had been bathing its picture for centuries.

When I read that passage, I thought of the parallel with literature and writing. Most of the writing you read, the words you see and hear every day, the vast mass of language you have been exposed to since childhood—most of those millions of words are served up in brown gravy, "every detail correct and complete, flat colors shaded slowly into each other." The tremendous edifice of "correct" grammar, the *whoms* and the *respectivelys*, the commas after *thus* and the clauses beginning with *notwithstanding*, the long unbroken paragraphs, the well-bred modifiers—brown gravy all of it, "flat, thin surfaces," "sentimental sobriety," it's all there. We get the truth, as Börne wrote, "killed, plucked, cut up, fried, and pickled." Everything is carefully prepared, revised almost before it has left the writer's mind, shaped in a mold, dressed up for company, brushed, combed, wearing a neat tie or a permanent wave.

I open this morning's paper and I read: "Senator Leverett Saltonstall, chairman of the Senate Armed Services Committee, took issue today with Senator Joseph R. McCarthy's charge that the recent ammunition investigation 'pointed out the general picture of treason.'" Has anyone ever *said* a sentence like that? It's English all right, nothing wrong with the grammar or anything else, but it's newspaper English. The full names and titles, the middle initial, "took issue with"— we read it every day and have long forgotten that it's all brown gravy. The world talks one way and writes another—and we don't care; we don't even feel it. Tired reporters quote half-sentences to us—"pointed out the general picture of treason" —and we don't even notice that such language can no longer be read aloud.

Try to read aloud these sentences from *Time*: "Choreographer (*The King and I, Call Me Madam*) Jerome Robbins, testified that he had joined the Communist party in 1944, quit it in 1947 a disillusioned man. He recalled that two other big names of the theater were members of his cell: Playwrights Jerome (*My Sister Eileen*) and Edward (*Those Endearing Young Charms*) Chodorov." You see how far removed this is from the way people talk? It's as artificial as Russian ballet. Maybe not brown gravy, but fancy sauce covering up all natural taste and flavor.

Or try the following: "This volume, described all too briefly, is a bold and impressive intellectual performance, highlighted especially by the author's logical skill, meticulous exegesis, familiarity with the natural sciences, conspicuous efforts to match the latter's theoretical sophistication, and wise insistence on the noncausal nature of his formulations." Beautiful English? Yes, in a way. It's brown gravy done to a T. The professor who wrote that book review for a scholarly journal, certainly "can write." Probably he felt a slight glow of pride when he had put that sentence on paper. But does it mean anything? Did he express his thoughts effectively? You think so? You may be right—if you are the kind of person who knows the Russian-ballet rules of academic book reviewing. Then you will have realized that the quoted sentence opens the final paragraph of the review, the one in which the reviewer tears the book to pieces, throws it on the floor and tramples on it with both feet. "But the performance is dimmed, I believe, . . ." he goes on—enumerating five deadly sins and ghastly mistakes the author has committed and adding sweetly that the book is excruciatingly dull, that much of its material has been copied from someone else, and that the author hasn't read the literature on his subject.

Brown gravy everywhere. I open a popular magazine and find an article that begins: "The ten-year-old girl laboriously repeated 'ball' after the teacher, then hesitantly underlined the word in a list on the blackboard. Three other children in the class . . ." What's wrong with that? you say. Nothing—nothing at all. But it's another formula that has become so common and standardized that we don't notice it any more. A magazine article has to start with a lead, an "incident," a "scene." Another Russian ballet. Why couldn't the writer have started, "This is a piece on the work with speech-handicapped children that's going on at the University of Wichita. When I got the assignment to do this article, I went out to Wichita . . ."? Oh, I know. You can't do that. It's against the rules. You can't shock people by admitting frankly what you are doing.

I open an English textbook (yes, it's still my pet "infuriating" one) and I read: "We continue to study our list of subtopics, but we can find no other desired additions or omissions. We are very careful in this final scrutiny because we know that a list of subtopics must be reasonably complete. . . ." Who are "we"? The authors? No: there's only one. An imaginary group? Writers in general? The people of the United States? No. You know as well as I do that "we" here means "you, the students." It's the educational "we"—closely related to the hospital "we" ("And how are we feeling today?")—one of the most nauseating specimens of brown gravy to be found in all literature.

And then there are always business letters and memos. People tell me that the old-fashioned type of business letter doesn't exist any more; "Yours of the 13th inst. rec'd and contents duly noted" supposedly has been relegated to the museum. Has it really? Then what about this authentic letter which was written and mailed just a few weeks ago?

An investigation of our records fails to show that we have ever received from your goodselves a report regarding the above captioned payment order. Inasmuch as our principals are anxious to know whether or not this payment has been made, we would appreciate your advising us, as soon as possible, the status of this order. If you have completed this payment, kindly advise us the date, and furnish us, if possible, with the payee's receipt. If, however, you have not as yet completed this payment, then kindly expedite same and advise us the reason for nonpayment. In the event that you did not execute this transfer because you did not receive our original instructions, then kindly accept this letter instead and endeavor to complete this remittance without further delay, under advice to us. . . .

And so forth. All of which, of course, is the brown-gravy way of saying "What about that remittance?" That would be undignified? Yes, of course. So are Van Gogh's pictures.

And advertising? The Madison Avenue Russian ballet? The world of solitary comparatives ("whiter," "fresher," "milder"); of the colossal overstatement ("doctors agree," "scientific tests prove"); of the arch reference ("another network," "the more expensive spread"); of the chummy assumption ("the little girl you love so much"); the world of "two short hours," "seven years of research," and "lifetime enjoyment"?

Brown gravy. Standard formulas, conventional ways of saying things, of naming things, of using language to make ideas conform. The English textbooks tell us about euphemisms and give examples like using *limbs* for *legs* or *passed away* for *died.* But the truth is that our whole conventional way of speaking and writing is one vast system of euphemisms; we don't talk about things as they really are and it would seem shocking if we did.

A few years ago Mary Martin sang in *South Pacific*: "If you'll excuse an expression I use, . . . I'm in love with a wonderful guy!" Think about that. It is startlingly true. We have come to the point where we have to apologize for saying we're in love.

You know about all that, really. There isn't anything new in what I am saying here—except that it just *might* give you the healthy shock that Van Gogh got when he saw that exhibition. I don't expect that to happen, but it *has* happened occasionally: I'll never forget the student who told me after one of my classes about a simple thought that had struck him; he had suddenly realized that it was "legal" to write plain talk.

Even if you do suddenly see the "brown gravy" that covers most writing, you'll find it hard to change your own habits. Don't kid yourself: it's not easy to speak and write good, strong English these days, to put sensible ideas into natural words. The pressure of the world around us is overwhelming. The morning paper, the incoming basket at the office, the lunch and dinner conversations are filled with weak, insincere talk—prefabricated, shoddy verbal material—the kind of stuff that seems to form itself automatically without thinking. Vague, meaningless phrases are on our lips or on paper way ahead of powerful, convincing words. Plain, truthful, personal language is the product of continuing daily renewed effort. It means work; it is a way of life.

Mechanical means can be a help in such an attempt to

change your habits, just as a calorie chart is a help in dieting or setup exercises are a help in keeping fit. That's why my readability formulas have been welcomed by many people: not because short words or short sentences are good in themselves, but because the effort of watching your language keeps you on your toes. Some time ago I drew up a list of ten such self-training exercises—arbitrary devices that will help you keep your language in shape. I *don't* recommend the permanent use of any of these exercises: it would be like trying to eat nothing but vitamin pills. But I know that they work if you take them "if and when needed."

Here they are:

1. Write an exercise, limiting your sentences to ten words.
2. Write an exercise, using one-syllable words only.
3. Write an exercise, expressing your ideas as much as possible in figures and proper names.
4. Write an exercise, using as many different punctuation marks as you can.
5. Write an exercise with a minimum of punctuation.
6. Write an exercise, expressing your ideas as much as possible by quoting what people *said*.
7. Write an exercise, using the first person as much as you can.
8. Write an exercise, using the second person as much as you can.
9. Write a short passage, and then rewrite it, using entirely different words.
10. Take fifteen minutes to think of as many new words and metaphors as you can.

Let me illustrate:

Limiting your sentences to ten words is not easy. Ten

words are fewer than you think. You can't write complex or compound sentences that way: you've got to break them up. Colons of course help; so do semicolons. Otherwise terse sentences look awfully choppy: you can see that for yourself. But look at the zip this exercise gives your language: it's like turning on the cold shower.

Or take the use of one-syllable words. (The word *syllable* has three syllables; too bad if you want to use it to show how the thing works.) It can be done, I tell you; try it. You will find that all thoughts can be told in short words. You can talk like that of God and the world; of time and space; of homes, cars, food, clothes, toys, and books; of men and—er, girls; of sons and—er, girls; of all things you know and, of course, of all things you *don't* know. Some times you will have to search for a word; or you will have to go out of your way to hunt for a phrase; but if you learn how to play this game, you can not be licked. It's fun; you will see.

Next, see what you can do with proper names and figures. Don't make your points in the abstract; tell people that your idea has been tried by Mrs. Thomas H. Friendly, of 62 Elm Street, Leftburgh, Ohio; she made 157 different tests and found that the thing worked in 84 per cent of the cases. She also rang in her neighbor, Mrs. Charles V. Unfriendly, who made 29 tests, with 64 per cent success. Mrs. Unfriendly wanted to go on but Mr. Unfriendly stopped her.

Next, start playing with punctuation. I wrote a whole chapter on that, so there's no need saying much about it here. Use exclamation points! Break up your declarative sentences into questions and answers. Don't write: "People were satisfied." Write: "Were people satisfied? Yes." Use dashes—use *italics* —vary your punctuation! Pepper your writing! Salt it! Why not? Let yourself go. And don't forget—there's always that most emphatic device of them all, the one-sentence paragraph:

It can't be overlooked.

Next, use a minimum of punctuation for a change. This means a diary-type, jotted-notes style—or else words tumbling out one after the other in unorthodox startling pressing emphatic urgency like an irrepressible overwhelming flood like a river like the Mississippi taking the reader along and not letting him go there is no stopping point and therefore there is also no point for escaping the argument don't give your reader pause pause to think pause to contradict you pause to come up with an answer pause to realize that you are using rhetoric rather than reason mind you I am not recommending this as a way of speaking or writing for any ordinary purposes these are exercises for you to limber up and see what you can do with language the English language has possibilities you never even thought of it's like eating a kind of food you never tasted before how do you like it you don't have to eat it all the time.

Or try using quoted dialogue. Most people shy away from using direct, quoted speech in their talking and writing. Why not try? Don't say that your neighbors came over last night and you had a lot of fun playing the new game, "Scrabble." Say it this way:

Ed came over last night while Elizabeth and I were playing Scrabble.

"What's this?" Ed asked.

"Why, haven't you heard of Scrabble?" I said. "It's the latest. We're nuts about it."

So Ed sat down and kibitzed. After three minutes he said: "This looks like fun. I'll get Mary over and let's have a game."

Well, we played until 2 A.M. "Why didn't I know about this before?" Ed said when they left . . .

Next. Experiment with the use of the first person. Say *I* as often as you can manage to bring up the subject—or *we* if you are writing as a member of a group or organization. Did you ever write the kind of report or scientific paper where you have to say "the writer" in referring to yourself? Then you know that there is no quicker and more efficient way to make your writing stilted and inhuman.

Exercise Number Eight: Use *you* to excess. Go all out speaking about your audience and writing about your reader. If you try hard, you can find a place for the second-person pronoun in practically every sentence you say or write.

Now comes Number Nine—a tough exercise but one that will teach you a lesson. Rewrite whatever you have written, using not a single one of the words you used the first time. This seems impossible but it can be done. You will learn that words and ideas are not the same and that every idea can be expressed in an infinite number of ways.

Let me illustrate with the last four sentences that I have written: This hard test is most instructive. Put something on paper, then do it over, changing each item of the vocabulary employed. Looks as if it could not work, but actually it's quite feasible. Moral: Vocabulary is different from thoughts; everything can be said in a limitless variety of words.

Finally: Use as many new words, metaphors, figures of speech as you can. Here you are on your own. Put your creativity to a test. Try coining new words—try a little "verbifying." You don't like this new word of mine? All right, make a better one. Think up some new metaphors—how good a poet are you? Say things as they have never been said before;

enrich the English language. This morning I thought of calling self-help books and articles "advice to the life-lorn." I rather like the term; I think it expresses the idea pretty well. You don't think much of it? Well, it's your move.

Don't misunderstand me. I am not saying that the way to improve your English is to work on these ten exercises. They are training devices; you can use them to keep yourself in trim. But the theme of this book is that communication cannot be learned by home study or by doing certain mechanical things at certain hours each day. Communication is life; making sense is a matter of learning new habits. You can learn it only by doing—like swimming, like driving a car, like playing golf, like running a business. It has been said a million times that public speaking can only be learned by public speaking, writing only by writing. Reading a book on the subject is often an attempt to escape that basic truth. It can't be done. There is no substitute for life.

For after all, communication is a tremendous, unfathomable mystery. You can sit down at home, think up a beautiful speech or article, rewrite it a dozen times, stuff it to the brim with brilliant ideas, startling facts, breath-taking beauty of language. Then it gets exposed to an audience and what happens? Absolutely nothing. Some intangible element is missing. Nobody is interested; nobody pays any attention to what you have said.

Why is this? Because all communication is a matter of the emotions. There is no such thing as pure, unadulterated thought; you can't put ideas or facts in words and simply hand them over to someone else. There must be some emotional bridge; something inside the other person must respond. Nobody can take in anything without at least a flicker of interest;

without that flicker of interest the words won't even register. And what is that flicker of interest? It's an emotion. If your words can't arouse that bare minimum of emotion, they are dead. They are as if they had never been spoken or written.

And so the real problem of communication is how to establish emotional contact with other people. You don't believe that? You don't think that applies to a legal opinion, a paper on theoretical physics, a cost estimate for the building of a new plant? I assure you that it does. Without emotional contact, without that flicker of interest that *must* be stirred, nothing can possibly have any effect.

And how do you establish emotional contact? By vocabulary? By grammar? By correct pronunciation? By spelling? Obviously not. Rather, by communicating your own interest in what you are talking about and in the people you are talking to. You have to be emotionally involved yourself. And that's why it doesn't do any good to simply repeat some facts you have collected. The formula is, Get the facts; forget them; then remember them again as you communicate them. Why must we forget them before we can use them in communication? Because we have to get emotionally involved. Something of ourselves must be made to stick to the facts before we give them to the audience. They must be dipped into our unconscious, the seat of our emotions, before they can be made to register.

But that's only half the job. To establish emotional contact, you must also involve the unconscious of the audience. Your words must somehow make *their* emotions come to the surface. You let down a bucket into your own unconscious, pull up the words you use, and address them to your audience; then, when the words have arrived at their destination, the audience must let down buckets into *their* unconscious and come up with some emotional response. Make them laugh, make them cry; or at least, make them get interested, prick up their ears, sit up and notice.

How can that be done? How can the emotions of your audience be put to work? There are only four ways of doing that—four alternatives that *must* be used by anyone who wants to tell anybody anything. You can either ask questions like Socrates and let the other person arrive at the solution by himself; or you can let him learn by demonstration or experience; or you can tell him something that happened; or you can tell him something that didn't happen but makes a good story. That's all. Your audience must get some emotional experience, either real or imaginary; without that, nothing you say will make the slightest difference.

Which means, in other words, that to communicate you must digress. Pure thought by itself does not communicate; there has to be some emotional material to carry it across. Strictly speaking, the emotional stuff is always a digression; but practically speaking, those digressions are more important than the main thought. Once I made a speech about book selection to a group of librarians. During my speech I happened to refer to a book I had read just the day before: *The Cry and the Covenant* by Morton Thompson. I expressed my enthusiasm for the book (a novel about the life of Semmelweis) and devoted a few sentences to it. Later I heard it was that digression that interested my audience most.

Another time, in a book of mine, I briefly mentioned that electric shock therapy was opposed by the original discoverer of insulin shock therapy, Dr. Manfred Sakel. Most of the letters I got from readers of that book dealt with that short, totally irrelevant paragraph.

People are afraid to digress. They think sticking to the point is a virtue. But is it? Or is it narrow-mindedness if you limit yourself strictly to the matter in hand and don't allow yourself to wander off into the byways? Remember the psychoanalytic technique of saying whatever comes to mind; remember that this is practically a definition of freedom of speech. Why curtail your own freedom? Why *not* talk about the irrelevant? How do you know it's irrelevant? Maybe it's the only thing you have said that will bear any fruit.

The truth is that you shy away from digressions because you shy away from *any* free, spontaneous talk and writing. You don't say or write what crosses your mind because you don't want your private thoughts to be seen or heard in public. You have trouble with speaking and writing for the simple reason that you are afraid to say what you think.

Learning to speak and write is like learning how to swim. You are afraid to leave the familiar solid ground under your feet and give yourself up to the new medium. Only when you have made the decision to let the water carry you, can you really begin to learn how to swim. Just so you have to trust yourself and the contact with your audience to carry you ahead and give you words to express your thoughts. Stick to a prepared manuscript and you'll never learn how to be a successful speaker. Stick to a narrow, point-by-point outline and you'll never learn how to write readable, interesting prose. You have to take the plunge first; you have to start by doing for the first time something that you think you cannot do.

All learning consists of doing something you are afraid to do. All self-improvement consists of the same thing. Emerson said we should do something we fear every day of our lives; hundreds of self-help writers have echoed his words. Do the thing you fear; practice and master the unpleasant, the embarrassing, the difficult; do what you don't like, what goes against the grain, what makes you feel uncomfortable. In a word, *Do what makes you self-conscious*; this is the golden rule of living.

Speaking and writing are the best proving grounds for the practice of that golden rule. From the first words we uttered as babies, to recitations in school, to written themes, to personal letters, to business letters, to speeches of all kinds, to conversation at parties, to writing for publication, to all the different kinds of spoken or written words our lives call forth— each new kind of communication starts with an awkward, stumbling, self-conscious, excruciatingly painful effort.

And now here we are grown up—supposedly fully able to speak and write our language. But are we? Actually each one of us spends his life on a small island of personal relationships, with a few people with whom we communicate without self-consciousness. Outside that small circle, all around that small island of ours, there is a vast sea of millions of people to whom we are afraid to talk, to write, to reveal any of our thoughts. Improving our English is a matter of overcoming self-consciousness throughout our lives.

On the small island that confines our personal lives there are our families, our relatives, our neighbors, our close friends, our business associates. At the edges of the island are people we know slightly, casual acquaintances, people we say hello to, chance encounters. And then there is the sea—the ocean of mankind. We are afraid to swim in that ocean, to talk to strangers, to persons of the opposite sex, to people younger than we are, to people older than we are, to the rich and important, to the poor and unimportant, to people with accents, to people with unfamiliar occupations, to the very learned, to the very ignorant, to children, to sick people, to foreigners—to everybody who doesn't inhabit our personal island.

And that's why the real trouble starts when we are called upon to make public speeches or write for publication. Then we are supposed to address ourselves to people we don't know—to large groups of unknowns who may be anybody. They may be like the people who live on our own little island, but they may also be utterly different. How can we know how to talk to them? We haven't had any practice; it's the first time we meet them.

To overcome that fear and self-consciousness we must forever work on enlarging our little personal islands. If we are not good at talking to children, we must seek opportunities of talking to children; if we are uncomfortable with total strangers, we must deliberately enter into conversations with strangers on buses and trains. We must become greedy for chances to talk and write—particularly to people that make us feel self-conscious. In meetings we must take part in the debate from the floor; at parties we must contribute actively to the general conversation. If we get excited about something in the paper we must write a letter to the editor; if we think of a plot for a short story we must write it and send it off.

It will be useless, of course, if we do all that speaking and writing without emotional involvement. Our feelings must get into our words, the more so the better. We can overcome self-consciousness only if we learn to talk freely about things that interest us and get us excited. To exchange the time of day with your mailman doesn't add much to your invisible island: find out whether he collects stamps, whether he has a favorite nephew, where he stands on baseball; then tell him about *your* hobby, *your* family, *your* interests.

The trouble with all of us is that we have gotten out of the habit of expressing our emotions. Human beings, like their evolutionary ancestors, are so designed by nature that every emotion should have an outward expression. An ape shows hunger, fear, pain, and rage on his face and with his whole body—as the biologist Walter B. Cannon has shown, he prepares himself automatically for fight or flight. Human beings have one more alternative: instead of fighting or fleeing they can respond to dangers and opportunities by communication. When something unexpected happens, they can jump, frown, shrug their shoulders, howl, clench their fists, get red in the face, break into a cold sweat, breathe heavily, or do a hundred other things that once were physical preparations for fight or flight; but they can also utter words. In fact, they *have* to utter words or they will immediately upset the natural balance between emotional intake and outgo.

Every day doctors discover new ailments that are psychosomatic—that is, that can be cured by restoring our balance of emotional communication. If we don't talk or write enough or with enough emotional warmth and sincerity, we'll sooner or later ruin our health or have a nervous breakdown.

The other day I took my small son to see a three-dimensional movie. It was a matinee and the theater was filled with children—children who whooped and yelled whenever a ball or a chair seemed to fly out of the three-dimensional screen directly at the audience. There was no inhibition of the slightest degree in the expression of the emotions of those children; they acted like healthy young animals and all the yelling and screaming probably did them a world of good. Grownups don't act that way any more; they behave themselves, they are dignified, they know how to hide their feelings. They don't scream with laughter, they don't slap their thighs, they don't shiver with excitement: they have learned to keep their emotions *inside*. And that's where they get ulcers and allergies or where they feel uncomfortable whenever they have to write a letter or make a speech.

No, learning how to make sense is not a matter of grammar, pronunciation, or vocabulary. In his famous comedy *Pygmalion*, Bernard Shaw maintained that an illiterate flower girl can be made indistinguishable from a duchess by training her habits of speech. Somehow this fairy tale has become part of the American Dream and we think that improving our diction will put us at the head of a million-dollar company. It isn't so. Vocabulary-building and correct grammar are *not* the road to success; the only key to better communication is flexibility, practice in communicating our true feelings to any kind of person, anywhere. If there isn't anybody who'll make you self-conscious if you meet him or her alone, then you can't possibly have any trouble speaking or writing to an audience.

That flexibility is only acquired by practice, by learning the habit of saying and writing things at the spur of the moment, in answer to the challenge of the situation before us. Mr. Hegarty, in his book on *How to Write a Speech*, tells of an occasion where he wore a red necktie to a meeting. Before he could say a word, a man in the audience called, "Ah, a guy with a red necktie!"

"Yes, a red necktie," Mr. Hegarty answered. Then he pulled the tie out of his vest and went on: "When they asked me to talk to this group they told me that you were a red-hot sales force. So I put on the hottest tie I have—I wore it to remind me to be good."

And John Crosby, writing his television column the day before the coronation of Queen Elizabeth II, was inspired to unusual heights of satire by the ridiculous horse race of the American networks to get the coronation films first. "Throughout the day," he quoted an NBC press release, "there will be bulletins on NBC-TV, reporting the progress of the networks' planes as they wing their way west with the coronation films." To which John Crosby added:

"Hot diggetty!"

This was the first time I ever saw the words "Hot diggetty!" in print. That's slang, you say: you are not *supposed* to use words like that for publication. I say, Nonsense. Honor to a man who dares to use the emotionally true words a situation calls for.

All of which means that we can best enlarge our personal islands by using the feedback principle. We can learn to talk to anybody by talking to all sorts of people at all sorts of occasions, saying whatever seems to be the thing to say at the moment. The second time will be easier than the first; the third time will be easier than the second. The moment will come when you think nothing of pulling your necktie out in front of an audience or appearing in print with the words "Hot diggetty!"

But the feedback principle is not the only way. There is also the opposite principle, the method of listening to yourself and letting your unconscious speak. There are hundreds of little languages that you can learn by talking to hundreds of different kinds of people; but there is also a universal language that is familiar to everybody. Our personal islands, as William James said, are connected through the ocean floor. When the tides of emotion rise high, we remember that universal language and have no trouble in speaking and writing to anybody. Earthquakes, floods, catastrophes of all kinds unite people and break down those unhappy inhibitions that keep us from talking freely to each other. War does that for us too—but fortunately also Christmas, happy events, and great celebrations. Then we let ourselves go—and suddenly we have no trouble any more with grammar, pronunciation, or vocabulary and, as if in a dream, we are changed into inspiring speakers and powerful writers.

At ordinary times, when nothing special happens to us, we somehow forget that universal language and stick to our civilized, timid, inhibited speech and writing. And we envy simple people who seem to know that universal language much better than we do.

Not long ago the president of a Brooklyn bank received three envelopes with $2,000 in small bills and this note:

Dear Mr. President:
  Last Thursday my daughter went to the bank to get some deposit slips for her father who is ill. On leaving, she noticed a pile of bills lying on the floor, which she foolishly picked up and took home. We knew nothing until a few days later when she told us because she is nervous. Believe me, she got killed plenty from us. We teach our child never take what is not yours, but she swears she find it and not steal it, so here is back your money and please don't make no trouble.
  For my girl is only fifteen years old.

Here it is, that universal language of mankind—complete with wrong tenses and a double negative, but every word coming straight from the heart. Can you learn to use the English language as effectively as the mother of that girl?

Perhaps. But that would mean a deep change in your whole being. You would have to become a different person.

In Dostoyevsky's *The Brothers Karamazov,* one of the characters describes Alyosha, the saintly one among the three brothers:

> Here is perhaps the one man in the world whom you might leave alone without a penny, in the center of an unknown city of a million inhabitants, and he would not come to harm, he would not die of cold and hunger, for he would be fed and sheltered at once; and if he were not, he would find a shelter for himself, and it would cost him no effort or humiliation. And to shelter him would be no burden, but, on the contrary, would probably be looked on as a pleasure.

Perhaps you would have to be like Alyosha Karamazov to be able to talk to anybody. Perhaps, to make sense to all people at all times, you would have to be a saint.

Appendix

A New Readability Formula

THE FOLLOWING IS AN EXPERIMENTAL formula to test readability. It is entirely different from my original formula, which was published in my book, *The Art of Plain Talk* (1946), and from the revised formula, published in my books, *The Art of Readable Writing* (1949) and *How to Test Readability* (1951).

"Readable," according to Webster, means "easy to read because interesting or pleasing." In other words, readability is what makes people like to read a piece of writing—or, for that matter, what makes people like to listen to it when it is spoken aloud.

Of course, readability is relative: what is readable for one person may be unreadable for the next one. However, a measurement formula disregards such differences, just as a thermometer disregards individual differences in "normal" temperature: it estimates readability for the mythical "average adult modern American reader."

This formula measures two elements of readability, which I have labeled *r* and *e* (meaning, roughly, "realism" and "communicative energy"). The *r* count estimates the quality discussed in Chapter 5, "Specify!"; the *e* count estimates the quality discussed in Chapter 6, "Poetry and Punctuation." Both are rough measures only, of course; they are designed to give an approximate idea of how the tested piece of writing ranks as to (*a*) realism, specificity, concreteness, and (*b*) energy, forceful delivery, vividness.

I applied this experimental formula to a wide variety of written materials and found the following pattern of typical scores:

Readability	Typical Material	*r* Score	*e* Score
High	Fiction, Drama	Over 25	Over 13
Medium	Journalism	15—25	7—13
Low	Academic, Professional	Under 15	Under 7

Both scores are figured "per 100 words." To test a piece of writing, you can therefore either count the scores in the whole text, divide by the number of words and multiply by 100; or—what is more convenient—you can take 100-word samples. Take these samples according to a predetermined random scheme, say, every fifth paragraph or every third page. All your samples should start at the beginning of a paragraph. However, introductory paragraphs are usually atypical and should be avoided.

In counting words, consider as one word every unit of letters or symbols that is surrounded by white space on both sides.

Now find the *r* score. It is a count of references to certain specified or individualized persons, things, or events.

Count the following:

(1) All proper names or titles of individual persons, places, events, organizations, things, or entities of any kind, e.g. *John, Mary, Smith, England, London, World War II*, the *1952 Election*, the *State Department, General Motors*, the *Empire*

State Building, the *New York Times, For Whom the Bell Tolls.* (Disregard articles preceding such words. Count separately each word that is part of the name or title, e.g. count *World War II* as 3 or *For Whom the Bell Tolls* as 5.) Count here particularly geographical names, e.g. *Broadway, Mississippi,* the *Pacific*; and the names of the days of the week, the months, and the seasons. Count also the names of the compass directions, *East, West, North,* and *South.*

(2) All nouns denoting human beings, including—in contrast to my earlier formulas—common-gender nouns, such as *secretary* or *employee.*

(3) All pronouns and pronominal adverbs referring to (*a*) previously *named* persons, places, things, events, or dates; or (*b*) human beings. In other words, count always the personal pronouns *I, myself, me, thee, thyself, you, yourself, we, ourselves, yourselves.* Count also *they, themselves, them,* whenever these pronouns refer to human beings; but count other neuter pronouns only if they refer to previously named things. For example, count the word *it* when it refers back to "the Waldorf-Astoria," but not when it refers back to "the hotel."

Pronominal adverbs are *here* and *there, now* and *then.* Again, these words are to be counted only when they refer to specified dates and places. Count also such words and expressions as *today, yesterday, tomorrow, this year, last week, next month, this morning,* etc., on the principle that they refer to specific points on the calendar or the clock.

Important: Count the word *you* also where it is only *implied* by the use of the imperative voice (e.g. *Don't forget!*). Similarly, count the implied word *I* in such expressions as *Thank you* or *Wish you were here.*

(4) All numbers and generally all words that can be ex-

pressed in figures, e.g. *twelve, first, double, dozen, half-mile, quintuplets.*

(5) All colors, that is, all words referring to a specific area of the spectrum, e.g. *green, yellowed, coal-black, red-faced.*

(6) All words specified or individualized by *preceding* words listed under (1), (2), (3), (4) or (5), either as adjectives, noun adjectives, possessive-case nouns, or possessive pronouns. In other words, *count everything specified by name, place, time, number, or color.* Count all the words contained in such a specified expression. Examples: *Mary's old fur coat* (count 4); *England's financial and economic problems* (5); the *General Motors annual report* (4); a *Broadway flop* (2); *last Monday's frightful weather* (4); *my social security card* (4); the *Waldorf-Astoria* (1) and *its famous guests* (3); *seven happy and eager kids* (5); a *gray flannel double-breasted suit* (4); *two loaves of bread* (4). Count such adjectives as *American* or *Italian* whenever they refer to place of origin, location, etc., but don't count words like *Negro* or *Jew* since they have no such denotation.

Count each word only once even if it comes under two or more of the listed categories.

As a general principle, remember that the *r* factor tests realism or concreteness by counting all references to one or more specific human beings and their attributes and possessions, plus all references to named or numbered things, locations on a map, dates on the calendar, times on the clock, and colors in the spectrum.

Next, find the *e* score. This is a count of directions for oral delivery—or, perhaps, cues or stage directions for a person who would want to read the piece of writing aloud. It includes indications of pauses, variations of pitch and stress, assumed voices of quoted speakers, and so on.

Count the following:

(1) All periods, colons, semicolons, dashes, and series of dots indicating a pause. (Commas, however, are never counted.)

(2) All question marks and exclamation points. Count two units for each of these: one for the pause, and one for the raise in pitch.

(3) All paragraph endings, indicating a longer-than-a-period pause, are counted as one extra unit in addition to the count of the period, question mark, or exclamation point concluding the paragraph.

(4) All devices for emphasis—italics, underlining, etc.—are counted as one unit for the whole expression italicized, underlined, etc., regardless of the number of words. Similarly, means of de-emphasis such as parentheses or double dashes are counted as one unit—not two—regardless of the number of words between the dashes or parentheses.

(5) All opening quotation marks when indicating the beginning of quoted speech (but not of quoted writing). Ending quotation marks are not to be counted; neither are repeated quotation marks following a speech tag like "he said." Example: *"Don't tell me," he said.* "I *know."* Count only the first quotation mark preceding "Don't."

(6) All apostrophes indicating contractions, e.g. *don't, we'll, that's.* Apostrophes in possessives—such as *the book's contents*—are not to be counted, however, since they don't indicate a contraction.

As a general principle, remember that the *e* factor tests vividness, forcefulness, energy of communication by counting cues for oral delivery. It counts the following units: ordinary pause (period, semicolon, colon, etc.); extra-long pause (paragraph); raise in pitch (question mark or exclamation point);

cue for stress (italics); cue for de-emphasis (parentheses, dashes); cue for quoted new speaker; contraction.

To show the application of the formula, let's take two extreme examples, one from Immanuel Kant's famously unreadable philosophy, the other from that classic of readability, Dickens' *David Copperfield*.

This is Kant:

> A good will is good not because of what it performs or effects, not by its aptness for the attainment of some proposed end, but simply by virtue of the volition, that is, it is good in itself, and considered by itself is to be esteemed much higher than all that can be brought about by it in favor of any inclination, nay, even of the sum total of all inclinations. Even if it should happen that, owing to special disfavor of fortune, or the niggardly provision of a stepmotherly nature, this will should wholly lack power to accomplish its purpose,/ if with its greatest efforts it should yet achieve nothing, and there should remain only the good will (not, to be sure, a mere wish, but the summoning of all means in our power), then, like a jewel, it would still shine by its own light, as a thing which has its whole value in itself.

Now let's test this piece of writing by our formula. We first count 100 words as a sample and find that there are 100 words up to the words "accomplish its purpose." Then we count the *r* score and find that it is 0: there is not a single one of the listed specified expressions. In other words, Kant deals here wholly with abstractions. Next, we count the *e* score and find that the score is 1 (the period after "inclinations.")

According to the formula, this example from Kant is therefore at the extreme end of unreadability.

Now let's take a sample from Dickens' *David Copperfield*:

> "Cheer up, sir," said Mrs. Crupp. "I can't abear to see you so, sir: I'm a mother myself."
>
> I did not quite perceive the application of this fact to *my*self, but I smiled on Mrs. Crupp, as benignly as was in my power.
>
> "Come, sir," said Mrs. Crupp. "Excuse me. I know what it is, sir. There's a lady in the case."
>
> "Mrs. Crupp?" I returned, reddening.
>
> "Oh, bless you! Keep a good heart, sir!" said Mrs. Crupp, nodding encouragement. "Never say die, sir! If She don't smile upon you, there's a many as will. You are a young gentleman/ to *be* smiled on, Mr. Copperfull, and you must learn your walue, sir."

To apply the formula, we again first count 100 words, which brings us up to "young gentleman." Now let's count the *r* score: *Cheer up* (implied *you*), *sir, Mrs. Crupp, I, you, sir, I'm, mother, myself, I, myself, I, Mrs. Crupp, my power, Come* (implied *you*), *sir, Mrs. Crupp, Excuse* (implied *you*), *me, I, sir, lady, Mrs. Crupp, I, reddening, you, Keep* (implied *you*), *sir, Mrs. Crupp, say* (implied *you*), *sir, She, you, You, gentleman.* The *r* score is therefore 41.

Next, the *e* score: Quotation marks at the opening of Mrs. Crupp's speech; period after "Mrs. Crupp"; contraction in "can't"; colon after "sir"; contraction in "I'm"; period after "myself"; paragraph after "myself"; stress on syllable *my* in "*my*self"; period after "power"; paragraph after "power"; quotation marks before "Come"; period after "Mrs. Crupp";

period after "me"; period after "sir"; contraction in "There's"; period after "case"; paragraph after "case"; quotation marks before "Mrs. Crupp"; question mark after "Mrs. Crupp" (count 2 units); period after "reddening"; paragraph after "reddening"; quotation marks before "Oh"; exclamation point after "you" (2 units); exclamation point after "sir" (2 units); period after "encouragement"; exclamation point after "sir" (2 units); contraction in "don't"; contraction in "there's"; period after "will." This adds up to an *e* score of 33.

With an *r* score of 41 and an *e* score of 33, this sample from Dickens is therefore extremely readable, as measured by the formula. Dealing with intimately personal matters and presented in vivid dialogue, it exemplifies the height of the two tested qualities, realism and energy.